Reality

Reforms

Your Life

Reality resets how purpose should be achieved. Synchronize the power of reality!

Dwayne Gavin

Cover designed by Sally Rice
Tallahassee, Florida
Edited by Jacqueline Harper
Brenda L. Smith Ph.D.

DG Publishing Press
dgpublishinghpress.com
850-566-8169

Dedication

I dedicate this book to Ms. Jacqueline Harper of Morgan, GA Retired in Quitman, GA. "Help those women that labour with us in the gospel." Truly, you have been the special helping hand constantly there for me endlessly with divine assignments, countless support, enthusiasm, patience and understanding. I wish to acknowledge you for all that you have done. Your spirit will always be evident for what you have done to embrace the challenges of Global Christian Church. In particular, your strong spirit has been evident as you have endured your own struggles. May God honor your kindness as I do! You exhibit the mannerism of the God sent.

Preface

Faith groups and faith healers have been with civilization before our time. The question for many is "Can the hand of God go beyond what man can do?" Orthodox and unorthodox people of faith hunger for an answer for God in terms of the meaning of God and the work of God. Seemingly, modern day practices are just illusions, and many faith leaders in their prophecy and prophecy projects are not relevant enough to come clean on the matter. Prophets and prophecy project God will interact with creation in the way that all people have no doubt about God. Many people use the name of God for wealth, some use the name of God for a weapon, and others use the name of God to silence people's free will and/or free mind! Could we be expired with God due to our lack of awareness of God and the meaning of God? It is said best among those that are closest to finding God that God is the Awakening for those who want understanding. Is it a universal truth, just as it has been since the formation of faith groups as well as the church, we too are living in the day in which God is constantly improving our awareness? Once people can replace their ignorance with awareness which equips them with understanding, recovers them from error, and empowers them with new born knowledge, the Awakening has come! Very few do it. A higher consciousness and a new reality seem not to be the challenge everyone accepts, but all may have been born prey to ignorance! Could it be that all people are part of higher God consciousness and thus, yearn to see God come out again and display unborn happenings which our eyes have not seen, our ears not heard, and our hearts not felt? As one biblical author and scholar has said,

"For having a zeal of God, but not according to knowledge. They being ignorant of God seek to establish it themselves." Seemingly, this notion has proved itself in every culture since civilization. Could this generation be different? Wow, just imagine the damage ignorance has placed on the subject of God and/or faith groups for such a long time! Certainly, being attuned with your inner self awakens you so that you straighten up your faith instead of those endless denominations popping out today doing it for you. The awakening of awareness, understanding, and knowledge is due to our being made in all power and intellect of the Creator; therefore, your brilliance is discovered considering that you find exceptional clarity about your inner self and its agility of intellect and intervention with God! So let us move forward with all truth turning over all those unturned pages, seeking to have new discoveries, and outpouring outcomes manifested by faith groups, believers, and Christians. Could it be that what we all want to know is knowable and the way thereof is shifting into a higher state of consciousness unborn that all may demonstrate God! God has your hands with which to work, your mind with which to inspire, and your faith with which to represent. Are we about to discover that God is within us and accept it? Studying the truths gathered in this book, you will likely expand your view and realize that reality depends on your identification. Reality is self analysis coming to a full circle by perception which can always change to a purer reality as your identification with everything escalates to new awareness. Changing your interpretation about everything also changes your reality about everything and ultimately, the results of your emotions, your feelings, and wellbeing. This compilation reports reality being the awakening truth discovered about oneself in consciousness.

Reality is a matter of how you perceive the world that you have imagined in your mind and heart. The burden of truth about oneself is to discover higher consciousness to recover oneself from the ills of society. Reality that embraces truth is the final distance of self awakening; thus, it is the inclination of awareness of things as they really are relative to literal and/or actual truth. All people having subjected themselves to this realization throughout history were those that mentally discovered the greatest sense of peace. Genuinely speaking, self awakening is the reflection of reality and the condition of comprehending the sum of that which can exist as literal truth; that which can be absolute; and that which can be real. In this book, the fundamentals are of such that components of reality are obtained as you gain knowledge of attributes about correction of self. Listed in this writing are concepts to help you gain totality of all things possessing actuality, existence, or essence. The underlined view to be discovered from reading this book is that insightfulness arises independent of abstract reasoning. The purpose for writing this book is to awake a conscious awareness of an adjustment to oneself and the environmental dictates in a fashion that releases incomparable satisfaction of instinctual needs.

Introduction

An awesome awareness and wisdom about getting to know yourself in ways that may propel you to a more meaningful life starts with your definition of reality. This self analysis makes you aware of yourself. As you examine the wisdom about basic reality in this book, my hope is that you become a more accomplished person. You may find this book to be your very own accumulation of insights that will help you as you begin to understand who you are and the qualities to change what you used to be. It is then that your life will begin to unfold many extraordinary yet successful outcomes. Hopefully, this increased understanding will help you position yourself in life with a clear direction, and to some degree, attain balance, power, and control. Self realization puts you on the path of success. Above all, there are specks of awareness in this book that will equip you with the knowing about yourself which will advance your identification of the fundamental laws of reality.

Contents

Part I

12 Fundamentals of Reality

Part II

Re-form Your Reality, Re-form Your Life.

About the Author

The Reverend Dr. Dwayne Gavin is the second of four children to Ms. Janis Gavin. He was born in Tallahassee, FL in 1971. He attended public schools in Tallahassee, FL and Atlanta GA. Born again into Christ, he united with the congregation of Greater Mount Zion P.B. Church at the age of 18. God called him into the Gospel Ministry at the age of 19. He attended Tallahassee Community College and Bethany Divinity College and Seminary, Dothan, AL (Albany-Center) in 1999.

He earned the Bachelor of Ministry, Master of Ministry, and Doctor of Theological Studies degrees. His pastorates include Piney Grove P.B. Church, Havana, FL; Mount Zion P.B. Church, Tallahassee, FL; Beulah M.B. Church, Quitman, GA from 2005 to 2011. He founded Dwayne Gavin Ministries Global Christian Church in Lake

Park, GA in 2011 and relocated it to Tallahassee, FL in 2012. He is currently the Senior Pastor of Global Christian Center. Dr. Gavin also served as an instructor at the Tallahassee Center for Biblical Studies where he taught Poetic Books of the Bible.

He is an accomplished, published author. His bestselling books Choose Your Life, Triumph, and Morality are sold nationally and internationally. Dr. Dwayne Gavin's books are sold at dwaynegavin.com, dgpublishingpress.com, Amazon.com, Barnes and Noble Book Store, Books-A-Million Online, Google Books, UK, Australia, India, North Africa, Canada and a number of other distributing agencies.

1

Reality

Reality reminds us of how to enhance ourselves in every way. The depth of higher morality is the result of reality. It is the tool that determines what life can be. There is no such thing as being bound to any aspect of your life should you realize that reality is subject to you.

The law of reality is
the notion that you
are incomplete of reality-
until you form an
internal dialogue.

You may change reality any time to a new reality just by acknowledging higher meaning of your life. Reality, therefore, carries you to all of your experiences and in some sure way determines many outcomes in your life. Your reality, which is reflected in every phase of your life, is very much visible in your character and attitude. Also, your actions are the influence of reality. The idea of being aware of your outcomes in life can be traced back to your reality. More reality is the factor considered in terms of maturing from basic stages of identification to a deeper agreement of beliefs with which to establish unity, peace, and well being.

Everything in your life is measured by your reality. Your decisions, attitude, and feelings trace back to your reality. Even, taking control of your morality is the work of identifying purer states of reality. Your reality positions you in relationships with others and yourself. To become aware of reality, you tend to handle better the details in your life.

You cannot obtain holistic peace without an internal dialogue with reality.

Thus, basic reality has a way of improving holistically every aspect of your life starting with your behavior, attitude, and well being. In a very subtle way, reality regulates the decisions you are making whether good or bad and happy or sad. It is important to know that your reality—being how you are processing and interacting with yourself, others, and the world— enables you to see the true reflection of your morality. One of the ways to becoming successful is to be realistic. Being realistic is to use reality to reach your goals in life. Outcomes in your life are associated with the reality of carefully assessing and, if necessary, adjusting the way you identify with everything to work itself into your mind to improve yourself.

Basic reality, therefore, suggests that you tend to express an awareness of things as they really are, no matter what you want it to be, expect it to be, or think it should be at anytime in your life. This does not exclude the fact that things can change drastically. Persons who are inclined to literal truth as it is in terms of persons and events are actually in my view, realists. It is biblical that everyone should be. A realist is one who uses reality, the truth, wherever it is whenever it shows up no matter what it costs to achieve. Realists are far and in between today! Although everyone wants to deal with a realist when it comes down to interacting with an ideal person, most people struggle with being real and transparent themselves.

Reality does awaken awareness of an adjustment to environmental demands in a manner that assures ultimate satisfaction of instinctual needs. How to regain control over your feelings in your life is very much the quality of realistic thinking. Likely, from time to time everyone needs to re-evaluate and realign his or her thinking to an unselfish use rather than always being right. Life tends to take on new meaning after one has gotten in touch with reality. Reality can be seen as a change of mind. A change of mind is the beginning of new emerging reality. As renewal is a matter of readjustment of your thinking, so are outcomes the result of new reality.

After you have learned how to identify properly your thoughts, perception, interpretation, and faith with new awareness, you have the formula for next level manifestations. Who does not want to be recreated to someone better than what you were a day ago? Everyone is striving for perfection even if it's just to do better the things that you have done and/or are doing right now! Phases of your life are advanced or retained due to reality awareness.

Your mental activity will determine where you are with reality in terms of the evidence in your life. Advancement in life is a matter of reality adjustment. In many ways, carefully analyzing your perception is a good thing to do because by observation of your thoughts you are certain to discover reality when corresponding with evidence in your life or evidence not appearing in your life. Reality is not to be confused with faith. The sum of reality is self awareness.

In many cases reality leads to self actualization and thought reconstruction. All of which are part of understanding how to recover yourself from an unrealistic view on everything including yourself. People having a willingness to handle the truth about themselves really maximize every moment in life. They see life as a reflection of themselves from a mental perspective of a creative artist which takes responsibility for everything being drafted in the field of the mind.

2

Identity

Identity is often a standard by which a thing is known. Often, reality comes down to an evaluation that is recognized by quality and condition of an identification of things. Unrestricting your identity is the element of change in your life. Applying yourself to observation in terms of how you are identifying and reacting to just about everything releases your reality about it in every way.

It is important to recognize that reality and identity are both factors of an inner working within your heart and mind. Your identity can speak about you in many ways to all those persons around you. That is noteworthy. Long before I recognized the value of understanding reality, I just fumbled through life with less than tough skin. It was afterwards that I realized reality has a way of enhancing my identity. In some sure way, it also works together with consciousness. Reality helps one identify with stages of awareness.

Awareness of obtaining
peace, happiness, and
calm feelings is
the work of identifying-

your internal image
of peaceful reality.

Equally important, reality gives you a healthy opinion of yourself and others which puts you on the road to becoming a realistic and accomplished person. The quality of being honest with your self is in accord with the reality that proves your character, personality, feelings, and relations. Correction on a "personal basis" tends to escalate with reality and higher awareness. Reality itself can take on infinite states.   Reality can never really be restricted; therefore, identification of things can take on new forms of identification daily. For example, reality adjusts the world in your mind; thus, the world changes when your reality of the world has been changed.

The essence of the developmental reality is a matter of attaining awareness during stages of your life. In a germane way, life can take on a different meaning after your reality about life takes on a different introspective. Reality can always advance your identification as it moves up the levels of awareness to identify with new understanding. It is necessary to know that reality is associated with what one believes to be true. I accept the fact that belief has a way of influencing reality to take on new discoveries of evidence.

The more expanded your beliefs are the broader your reality becomes. The whole idea about expanded reality is that you recognize that your life is either driven by your beliefs and they give life to your reality or that there is no evidence that motivates your inner self.

I suggest that you believe the first. I have discovered that new beliefs open up new awareness and new awareness opens up new reality. Even at the level of the moral arch, it bends with reality. Therefore, reality creates supernatural potential equivalent to energy that can empower your perspective about life. There comes along with new reality new emotions and new gratified well-being. Reality alignment is the bridge of transformation into next dimensions in your life. Often gaps in your understanding are sealed after you realize that you are the creator of your reality.

Thus, a renewed reality is a renewed spirituality. Neither can a life of spirituality be separated from a life of reality nor a life of reality separated from a life of spirituality. As with the notion of reality, the essence of your character is the reflection of your reality.

The same applies with spirituality. The core expression of spirituality is morality. Reality, in a spiritual sense, brings you the same result that religion offers— understanding! Just as spirituality enlightens you so does reality. They both identify perception alignment. Moreover, both have attempted to construct a universal point of view to establish awareness misalignment. Reality like religion is designed to ensure peace, rest, and well being with an assurance that provides clarity. Be realistic with yourself in terms of exploring all the facts about your life. There is a real way to find out all that you want to discover about yourself and life. I do enter this rest as bringing myself to a state of readiness to identify certain truths that I am withholding from self and others in the grand scheme of things.

I am sure that you can identify with me here. The truth about self will always be present when you are ready to face self. There are too many people today afraid to come clean with themselves which leads to some of the reasons for many mental disorders. Reality is part of the solution to the healing ministry needed for so many people. Only by being real with yourself can you begin to interpret your life differently. Reality, when corrected, assists in the reconciliation process in spirituality.

No matter the grievance in your life, a new reality can reshape your life and world view. Lastly, your reality is a definition of what you understand.

3

Awareness

It is pertinent that some emphasis be placed on awareness. We as human beings derive our morality from the reality of our awareness. It is equally important to understand how character develops if we are to come to grips with any advanced measures to ensure reform and progression to human character at its best quality.

Realistically speaking, I have been involved with how human beings can extend their intelligence to a grander reality for much needed reform should we someday display our "best" virtuous behavior. Levels of awareness today have to improve for there to be transcendence as we age. Awareness develops around understanding of how to interpret things in terms of reality. As you know, many have given reality to faith groups to correct the view of right and wrong.

Increasingly, political correctness and civil rights are racing to take the place of faith. Awareness is not prejudicial; it is not restricted to any field. It opens up in the political arena like it does in the religious arena. There should not be any contrast to awareness in terms of the arena in which it is present. Jesus used reality to provide you, His follower, insight and self awareness.

Often, He used a parable to establish reality. To add a thought, Jesus used the term "The kingdom of Heaven is like unto…" so that He could expand awareness. There are notable aims that Jesus Christ applied for the purpose of equipping His followers as He prepared His disciples to embrace new reality and new awareness about everything that He taught them. Often, His message embraced faith, reality, and awareness. Jesus' teaching method is the action of proliferating awareness of the reality of eternity.

Certainly, the eternal truth is that the world changes when human beings' faith, reality, and awareness of the imagined world take on change. In a very real way, there is no way reality can be excluded from our intelligence. Awareness is the total essence, which can be interpreted as the

source of human being intelligence.
Without an internal
dialogue in your life,
you leave out
awareness
therefore, depleting
your life of a true and
purposeful reality.

In terms of awareness and reality, there are present options instead of futuristic scientific events to explain many aspects of the world. The element of time must not be the only instrument to construct the identity of life. Instead, reality, faith, and awareness must be equally revered. Time is a matter inclusive of reality. The prerequisites to achieving purer awareness are observation, reality, awareness, and the inner self finding a new way of perceiving life. Reality must be engaged a lifetime in terms of exploring awareness to discover the technology needed in a modern world. Doing so increases new awareness. Repositioning from one state of reality to another escalated state of reality is the outcome of grander awareness. Alterations of reality trace back to a heightened consciousness.

This inner power can perfect your lives as long as you are shedding fragile reality which propels to grander realities. The greatest thinkers of old were in such agreement with this notion that they experienced fusions of miraculous ability to demonstrate awesome happenings that we know and read about today. Reality is challenging to people that fear it!

For there to be purer reality inspired

to enhance the way that you are cooperating with life, you must assume the responsibility of being aided by awareness of the Spirit of life. Basic reality creates majestic levels of change and, therefore, the source for behaving and interacting cordially with all things. To fully awaken to reality is not the work of medicine and drugs, but deeply tapping into the inner self and its divine strength. This maturity is the very work needed in the transition of the foundation for reformed life because it provides well being in a lasting way.

It is worth examining closer in terms of having progression reflected before your eyes. In order that you reach your potential, you will have to revisit your reality. It is then that reality guides you in ways that holistically improve your being. I might add, this reality awakens within you new perspective. To put it simply, reality is clarity. Reality leads us to acting intelligently. The changes that occur with expanding your reality are the result of a shift in consciousness that is self-assuring as you reach new truth. Reality awareness positions your potential.

Climbing the height of reality is a journey that requires letting your mind evolve instead of a closing of it at any time. When you encounter change, your reality demands an inner choice of new awareness to indwell you. Keep in mind that your choice of reality will determine your quality of life.

Reform Your Reality Reform Your Life

4

Certainty

All though we live with partial reality until it collapses to a higher identification leading to new reality, what is certain is that every breath we take is fresh and new. This gives rise to the type of reality that is renewing and certain. At any moment, reality can be renewable.

This is the one thing that is certain.

Certainty seems to be an absolute term, and the reason for it might be that anything doubtful impedes new reality. It's important to understand that reality itself is not a definite fix. Instead, it takes on infinite presence when it is asked to replenish. Thus, it makes new awareness.

This is certain when it comes to starting reality over. The renewability of reality is certain. Being certain about reality can only be interpreted that reality is the act of renewing or the state of having been renewed after you have taken on new identifications. By all means, of course, reality can be void in a closed mind, but it is certain that reality comes to dissolve that which is void to the mind.

When it comes to being certain, the notion to grasp is something clearly established or proven. I choose to point out those traits on the subject of what I term to be "certain about reality." One day while reading the Bible, I came upon an assuring passage which read, "Eyes hath not seen, neither ears hath heard and nor has it entered in the hearts of man those things which God has prepared for them that love Him." For me, I became intrigued by what I could term "certain."

What I have discovered is that certainty is both that which is visible and invisible. For years, many people have indisputably doubted those things seemingly invisible, but now it's time to recover the reality that all things are invisible before they become visible. It is just a matter of how you identify the invisible and thus, your reality about it. What is definite and absolute about the invisible is that everything starts from the realm of the invisible: Those things new to our eyes having not seen, new to our ears having not heard, and new to our hearts having not felt are definitely sure to come or to happen. The invisible is all that is, all that has been, all that can be, and all that can ever be. It is both the first and last, the beginning and ending range of possibilities including unborn and eternal. Another word for the invisible is spirit and/or creation. This is the manner in which reality is renewing and technology, innovation, and intelligence come into the world through all of us, even God.

Certainty is the reality that beyond doubt or question, the invisible is not separate from the visible; rather both visible and invisible are reflections of one another in realm only. Both visible and invisible realms rest in reality so there is no room for anyone to doubt their existence. I suggest that anyone with a realistic view point about each phenomenon not try to assume that having or showing no confidence to identify with both realms specify their existence in an uncertain form of dogma. There is in many cases identification of both visible and invisible realms either known or not mentioned, perceptible or not noticeable; therefore, it is safe to keep an open mind to the possibility that all things are certainly possible. This is the best reality.

In a very particular way, certainty can mean freedom from doubt. Being certain is very closely akin to faith. The difference is that natural certainty is based on what the eyes can see, the ears can hear, and the heart can feel in contrast to the invisible being evident beyond what the eyes have seen, the ears have heard, and the heart has felt. I advise that one sees both realms as mere reflection of the one presence. Certainty implies a thorough consideration of evidence. Some only want to define evidence as being visible, but no one can deny that the visible comes from the invisible until it reaches the visible realm in manifestation. Unless we see the invisible and visible realms alike as a pool of possibility coming out from infinite potentiality, we may not ever grasp the powerful biblical statement about that which is to come.

Should you have new hope about invisible things you may not ever use your fullest potential of being a possibility in the world. It would be most rewarding in every facet of the world should you turn off your light of possibility and potentiality so that the world can see the phenomenon of your being born to inspire another to reach greatness. When it comes to certainty, your mind can wrap itself around the invisible. Interestingly, that which is worth knowing is the fact that there is a conscious within you that you are not able to see, but it definitely is there. Just as the breath that you breathe is also certain. There also are things that you may not be able to understand without all the clarity that you need, but try not to form closed-minded conclusions about that which is certain.

The greater role of certainty seems to be clarity. Certainly, there is nothing that can reward you more than understanding. It is always less than possible to achieve clarity until the restraints of doubt, fear, and suspicion have been removed. These little plagues have caused people to stray from the path that leads to certainty.

Should there be
an absence of your
internal dialogue with
which to include
holistically the glimpse
of reality containing
a mental image of
lasting satisfaction,
certainty seems vague.

5

Detect Illusions

There will be something you need to face in order that you become free of unreality. Most of the time a hindrance seems to get in your way of making the choice to be free of unreality. That something is fear. False evidence appearing real leads you away from reality.

Detouring from false evidence helps you to live happily. Vast freedom of your mind encompassing reality independent of false evidence provides you real happiness. Reflective of reality is the wholesomeness that makes you happy. The reality of morality is the notion of replacing false evidence with truth. Before I realized that false evidence was the plague keeping me deficient of reality, I wondered if a happy life could be attainable.

A few encounters with delusion and defeat helped me to see that false evidence was the cause. I decided that if liberating reality was to be attained, I had to erase the false evidence appearing real making me believe that that was true. I had to realize that I was making myself believe things that were simply not proven. Thus, they were illusions and not true.

I had to stop making myself believe things that either did not exist or that I needed to face and later come to grips with, thus accepting things for what they were, were not, are and are not. Certainly, if anything existed, I was the one creating its existence or not willing to face reality of that which existed not. There were simply just too many imaginary things.

I tell myself often, "Sir, do not make things something that are nothing. Because when you do, you are leading yourself away from reality." This reminds me that unreality plagues me and, if I am not in control of what I sometimes determine as false evidence created by my imagination, then I am in a state opposite of reality. All unreality is keeping the truth from being presented.

My perception of life makes it happy or unhappy for me. Another change that shows up when you erase false evidence appearing real is that you begin to appreciate life. Your life takes on a new meaning; therefore, you start to comprehend the value and worth of a life of happiness. It is then that your new reality of gratitude appears. Happiness is not the result of removing fear of false evidence. Reality is the answer to overcoming the false evidence in your life.

Setback to your happiness is due to false evidence your personality accepts as truth. Your unreality is the object that must be examined for there to be any meaningful happiness in your life.

Reality is the essence of
truth and no matter where
it applies in your life, the
internal dialogue of self
reasoning brings forth
clarity of unreality.

Each minute of accepting false evidence in your life suppresses reality. I now keep in my mind that reality heals me mentally, emotionally, and physically. Values of people that are realistic are simple. People who face reality are happier than people who do not. I have learned to face reality and to follow it. They also do not prolong going beyond fear wherever it is necessary to attain happiness. There is a particular formula for happiness, reality!

There is a particular requirement for reality—remove false evidence in your life. It is simple; false evidence is unreality and a cancer to reality. Some major decisions are part of facing reality. If you place your decisions on anything other than choosing to face your fear, you will eventually realize that you are avoiding reality.

At the core of our reality, there lies an awesome truth about healing. That truth is being free from the fear of false evidence appearing real. I believe that you will never regret making the choice to rid yourself from all of the imaginary foes that you make part of your life when you have followed unreality. Consequently, you feel affirmed because you made the choice to follow the liberation of reality which detached you from fear.

The notion of being totally free from unreality makes your life into what you hope it to be. Thinking patterns that will reward you with peace and liberation are those that can handle reality. Persons free to see all the beauty of reality are people who inhabit happiness. Happiness is not a technique; it is a daily practice of facing reality. There is no reason for anyone to be unhappy. Just by being responsible for your own reality of the world gives you the right to choose the world that you perceive.

There is a Bible verse that I mention almost each time that I write that is so intriguing to me: "God has set the world within the heart of man…." It is your world to shape. Learn to be the greatest influence of your world and the greatest contributor in the world by understanding the reality of your mind. Reality is always available.

Your happiness is constantly present with reality; therefore, when the next obstacle of false evidence appearing real makes itself present in your life just dissolve it with the reality of facing whatever seems inevitable. To some degree, false evidence will often exist wherever you have not been realistic and have not explored. It is important for you to understand that expanding your reality is accepting being unconditionally unafraid to face all of your fears, knowing what lies beyond those things that you feared is reality or triumph.

Facing reality is the quest for peace, and the discovery of reality is knowing that you cannot afford unreality. The thought of being doomed by unreality is tormenting. Reality is a practice that can provide you a happy mindset. Reality conditions your thoughts to be thoughts that are pure, thoughts that are not bound to false evidence, thoughts that are honest, thoughts that are not fearful, and thoughts that are not partial.

The universal cure for unreality is the reality that erases false evidence appearing real. The key to a miraculous life is recognizing that you are the reality of your thoughts. It makes sure that your thoughts are not saturated with fear and/or false evidence. Learn to face whatever you fear and become willing to go beyond every boundary posing as fear. After doing this for some time, you will realize that false evidence appearing real was just a disguise of your fearful reflections about the unknown. In some divine way, reality provides knowing! You can know everything that you need to know or want to know just by facing reality.

Reform Your Reality Reform Your Life

6

Knowing

Knowing is accepting reality transferred from the state in which a person is unrestricted, unbound, and illimitable to boundaries posing as "final." The more inclined you are to reality the more you will discover knowing. There are many traps set to keep you away from knowing.

Unreality can be categorized among limitations, restrictions, mind control, boundaries, and death. All these barriers hold certain mysteries that can only be released as you move ahead to go beyond them. What you will receive as new awareness is new truth and knowing. Knowing is truth! There in the Bible is a powerful saying: "The truth shall make you free." I agree indeed that you become free from unreality, free from being restricted, free from being limited, free from being bound, free from death, and free from fear.

Only a deliberate conscious erases unreality, collapses fear, and hands over knowing. I try to be this way. The understanding of awareness gained through experience, all that is imagined to be concluded, is the brand I am addressing here as knowing. You should not conclude anything until after you have experienced it.

Should you conclude those untaken journeys, experiences not had, and boundaries never crossed, you cannot truthfully know all there is to know about your lack of experiences. Knowing is born when you delve deeper than normal into the infinite pool of limitlessness.

There really can be no limit to absolute knowing unless you restrict yourself from going beyond all parts of your life. The infinite knower in you always wraps its faith around fear of the unknown. Your knowing that the truth about the unknown, being your refusal to have a knowable experience because you fear knowing the absolute truth, may be because it is either you do not want to know it or you are not ready to accept it. It is always one or the other. Handling the truth is not as easy as is expecting to receive it. Therefore, knowing is a special calling for certain people who are non-partial to everything. Life is no exception to that partiality. Realistic minded people live being adaptable, flexible, and adjustable to all things because they have accepted life as an experience impermanent.

Often, I have had to rethink the meaning of life each time that I was challenged to adapt to impermanence. As a matter of fact, it is noted that knowing comes as the result of erasing mistakes in mental activity in consciousness; therefore, having found possession of absolute truth, one can no longer be denied absolute reality. I have long discovered that reality equates to truth in terms of the aphorism we have always heard, "Wake up to reality." This implies that one should never hesitate to acknowledge the facts about life at all time.

Your internal dialogue offers knowing. It is the dialogue of self analysis presenting all that occurred within your mind.

I am suggesting that you admit to yourself those certainties and uncertainties about all things as they really exist. Thus, reality is to be seen as truth. Knowing cannot be confused with ignorance. Once you accept the true reality about how things work in your life, you are no longer ignorant to them.

I must say, awareness of truth has to be accepted before any reality of truth will come. It is essential to know that awareness and understanding come on their own schedule in everyone's life, and no two people consistently reach absolute reality simultaneously. It is wise for all persons to become people of knowing. I am certain that the culture will take on this perspective generation by generation. Knowing is not an awareness that comes all at once, rather it comes one encounter after the next. So do not confuse the capacity of knowing with your brilliance as a human being.

Chances are that everything that you need to know will find you. Looking for mistakes in consciousness often accelerates your knowing. Just think about it. The best possible way to accelerate your knowing is as simple as observing your mistakes, facing reality, and continuing to adjust, adapt, and rethink errors that you make. This is very much a recipe for growth in human development. Do you think so? Well, it can be said growth is motivated by knowing and therefore, knowing expands growth. Begin to realize that at any time in your life that you are always interacting with all things so that you can either be taught or you are being evaluated. No matter the one, the observation is to realize that knowing is seeking you.

During those seasons of being taught and/or being evaluated, you are not being judged; instead, reality is pursuing you just as much as you need to pay attention to it. If you can see it this way, you bring yourself new awareness that may offer heightened discoveries. At this level of consciousness, reality equips you with a self - actualizing moment. Thus, clarity about yourself is attained and often leads to change of behavior better than your previous behavior.

Have you ever wondered what may be the answer to all things? I have. Learning is the answer to all things! First, learning paves the path to knowing. Second, learning is the process of acquiring experience with knowledge or identification of knowledge. Next, it implies a solution to correct unreality which is defined as an answer. Last the result of learning is to fix in the mind or memory mistakes due to lack of awareness. Learning inspires certain behavior modifications as do reality. It is almost erroneous not to classify learning as a branch of reality. In a case where lack of reality applies, so much falls to error resulting from defective judgment.

A misconception or misunderstanding always precedes reality and therefore, reality has to be seen as learning to accept truth. In the final analysis, knowing is equivalent to consciousness. At this level, knowing embraces both awareness and clarity. Without knowing, there can be little clarity, if any, and little awareness, if any; but when knowing is present, there can be no doubt that clarity and awareness about ultimate reality are evident.

The essence of knowing is that it fills your heart with assurance and your mind with confidence. To add a thought, during the process of becoming aware of reality, one gains clear understanding of himself which clearly brings oneself to ultimate understanding.

A change of understanding, therefore, is the transformation of lack of knowing to complete insightfulness. The only aspect of knowing which remains uncertain is the next minute and what it may manifest for you. Chances are that life is defined by this sole uncertainty because all human beings are driven by its curiosity.

7

Insightfulness

We are people, contrary to all the various notions out there to entice us to see ourselves as standards, political parties, logos, situations, beliefs, etc. Therefore, the right assessment about any human being victim to those affiliations aforementioned suggests that one embraces an awareness of recovered reality to equip oneself with a knowledge that penetrates all those images out there that deceive successful fundamentals of reality. Insightfulness is the capacity to discern the true essence of reality and contributes to progressive reality. The reality associated with its insightfulness about the nature of heightened human needs leads to successful outcomes. While insightfulness is discernment, it prevents error. Error is a catastrophe. Most times it delays the progression of happiness. As I have experienced, operating in error psychologically causes anxiety eventually.

Over a period of time, when you have operated in error without being aware of functioning in error, you, for the most part, detach from true reality; thus, your goals escape you, and you with some feelings for the most part are constantly disappointed. Prolonged psychological error works on your patience and deflates your positive attitude. During the process of operating in psychological error, everything that you hoped for seemingly fleets your reach; thus, you emotionally feel excluded from success. What is more, your morality of joy feels like a strand of thread. Here is where insightfulness is a saving grace. Insightfulness is at the core of reality. It brings again new joy that breaks the unhappiness of operating in error.

Insightful reality is waking up to truth no matter all of the ways social status, logos, standards, education, cultural beliefs, and political gurus twist unreality with attempts to establish wealth and/or prosperity. Insightful reality suggests that you not calculate riches as tangibility; instead, calculate them free of availing truth that enlightens your heart from deceptive devices psychologically, thus, ruining your advancement of the real fairness pertaining to achievement and personal growth. All the greatest teachers that have ever been in the world discovered the one authentic aspect about insightfulness—*going within*. It's just a simple principle that suggests that you apply keen observation to arrive within rather than on the surface of a matter.

Going beyond the status quo of things interprets the source of its creation. We all get better outcomes from day to day should we realize the importance of possessing insightfulness that provides the beginning wisdom of all matters. There are countless times in one's life that require insightfulness to be considered: for example, at which time one is presented an unforeseen circumstance, especially in the case when a decision has to be made instantly! We all face the unseen in our lives. So therefore, insightfulness about how to decide on what you do not know values above critical thinking. Thus, insightfulness is the wisdom to discern both the beginning and ending range of possibilities.

With this in mind, insightfulness is very much a treasure to have. It is not enough for the mystics to engage themselves with this manner of awareness; it has to become the beginning of your ways should you ever master the successful fundamental of reality. I have seen so many people confuse instinct with insight. When it comes to success the two are concepts that get misplaced often due to time and chance which happens serendipitously. What I have discovered about myself when I come to decisions in my life is insightfulness serves me best. When it comes to my personal feelings, instinct prompts me to arise from a response to individual stimuli. On the one hand, insightfulness is a discerner of thoughts, and the other instinct is spontaneous thought, even effortless thought. Discernment is designed to position your thoughts. You can have ten thousand thoughts running through your mind during the span of a day, but with careful observation to discern those thoughts, you can still be clueless. I might add it is just a matter of prioritizing insightfulness and instinct as you approach the attitude of successful reality.

Your goal to ultimate outcomes in your life should start with developing an observation behavior, and it should be the response to any uncertainty in your life. By so doing, you can develop discernment that isn't an inborn pattern of behavior that is characteristic. Thus, it becomes a powerful motivation or impulse, even an innate capability or aptitude that works for you miraculously.

Success depends on your being deeply filled and/or impelled from within discernment. Have you ever asked yourself why am I not reaching my ultimate goals as I envisioned meeting them? Most successful people find the answer on the pathway to success that observing things instead of participating in everything is the secret principle to the top. All successful people have discovered that success leaves a trace. Three of those traces for me have been developing a perfect attitude about everything that happens along the journey, coming face to face with reality always never viewing it as a second best option, and making discernment my option before moving too fast on decisions. Instead of participating with everything, choose to observe all things without reacting to everything. Successful people have tough skin! These traces of successful reality are attached to the abundant outcome of many people. Clearly, success is anchored in the word *observe*.

Many centuries ago, great emphasis was placed upon specific observers and their abilities to invent. Today, the notion still applies although in the West little attention is applied to inner observation since it's so closely associated with the concept of meditation, which it left to the hands of religion.

One trace biblically noted for the

usage of the point of observing can be found in the manuscript of Joshua written 1451 B.C. Largely, the beginning of the manuscript pointed out the wisdom of being a successor. The key tone of the manuscript is success by observing how to follow through and do those things which he was instructed. Also, the manuscript pointed out how his prosperity was a result of his observing his attitude and courage. I, therefore, conclude that observation is the beginning of discernment, and success comes through one's insightfulness. When you add discernment to your techniques of success, your successful fundamentals of reality can reward you by propelling you to reach desired outcomes in a more accelerative fashion.

Insightfulness is released
from your internal dialogue

that presents reality.

8

Wisdom

The reality of wisdom seemingly is esoteric. What makes it so rare is it isn't associated with educational dynamics only; learning is the whole matter. Instead, wisdom is more the manner of observing that which actualizes considerably everything. It's an infinite awareness. It does, however, come through experience, education, and conceptualization, but it does not come from those things. It is above those fundamentals and, therefore, dwells with absolute awareness handing down understanding that births knowledge and experimentation. To put it simply, the reality of wisdom is above mental fabrication; it's to be understood as mental creation!

Consider wisdom to be the beginning possession of the matchless course of action embodied with insightful knowing and all encompassing awareness. One with an ability to discern from beginning to ending and starting to finishing possesses wisdom. *Wisdom does for you a number of things, such as* reveals what is to be understood at a particular time if you are open to direction; releases excellent counsel; finds knowledge; imparts instructions; increases learning; multiplies prosperity; and prepares success. Does it come to your mind at anytime how do I do this or that so that I achieve the best possible outcome? If so, at that time, wisdom is what you crave in that moment. Everyone needs wisdom at some point in his life. Too many times, the absence of wisdom in one's life results in less favorable outcomes. What I have learned about wisdom is it tends to produce substance and treasures and blessings without sorrows.

There is a series of scriptures in the Bible about wisdom that reminds me of it mostly; " I was set up from everlasting, from the beginning, or ever the earth was...For whoso findeth me findeth life, and shall obtain favor...but he that transgresses against me injures his soul." I am reminded at all times the depth and/or volume of research that needs to go into decision making and choices because of this heightened truth pertaining to wisdom.

Should anyone apply wisdom in his/her life, abundant outcomes are certain. I have been intrigued by leadership ever since I did know how to recognize it. It is because leaders possess the wisdom to disarm doubt in the minds of those whom they lead. Soon I realized that I was attracted to wisdom and I discovered that I would need it.

Wisdom is a successful fundamental of reality. Living in a modern day global community demands that wisdom be out front in every aspect of one's life. So many things depend on wisdom in terms of outcomes desired. In many phases of my life where there was an absence of wisdom, I have had to pay dearly the consequences of my ignorance. It is true in my life that when I possessed wisdom to do certain things, the outcome was favorable which resulted in my not needing to be corrected. I seem to pray when there is need for correction.

Wisdom is important in your life. Remember the words about wisdom, "By me kings reign, and princes decree justice; By me princes rule, and nobles, even all the judges of the earth; Riches and honor are with me; durable riches and righteousness. I am the possession of God, the beginning!" Your goals are waiting for wisdom to accomplish them. It shall do just that! Everyone that sees the reality of wisdom being essential understands that waking up to the beginning of excellence is the sum of wisdom. Wisdom is the same as establishing dominion with tactful information. It works as power with insurmountable insightfulness to influence, achieve, and obtain favor with God and people. The knowledge released by wisdom is the creation of holistic wealth, such as, money, well-being, and status. Wisdom is the foundation of all lasting abundance. Over the periods of history, the reality of wisdom has impacted people and their outcomes tremendously.

Some successful examples include, on the one hand, wisdom which is responsible for inseparable friendships, self preservation, religious promotion, honor and increase; and on the other hand, a lack of wisdom applied in context with reality is the cause of setbacks, demotion, destruction, war, unhappiness, ruin, suffering, and death. There is only one way to sum the reality of wisdom. It's an infinite knower! Therefore, the reality of wisdom cannot be concluded; however, it is safe to treasure the reality of the best awareness for all matters. There is nothing better for man to possess than an inner depth of the reality of wisdom.

Reality is the result of
wisdom formed by
your internal dialogue.

Reform Your Reality Reform Your Life

9

Human Being

It is important that everyone realizes what it means to be human when it comes to reality. Thus, the subject is most controversial among various possibilities and/or outcomes associated with failure. With this being said, I propose that we take another look at what it means to be a human being. Mostly, people associate being human as limited to infinite consciousness, but there are people who associate human being with having the potential of reaching infinite consciousness. Interestingly, people in the West are more inclined to take the first point of view to be more centered; whereas, people in the East are closer to accept the second point of view to be more accurate. Who really knows?

There are supporting facts that increase awareness of human being developing supernatural vibrations in consciousness, and there are countless statements from the scientific community to embrace the notion human beings do not use one third of their brain power. It is reported that there is enough electricity in the human being's brain to ignite one of the fairly large cities in the U.S. Does this mean that people have minimum or maximum abilities? What it suggests is the amount of brain energy that people use is individual. Our brain is a field of potential. Limited or infinite potential is determined by the individual. If one wants to endeavor to reach infinite consciousness, it is an option; and if one does not choose to reach limited consciousness, it's an option. So, what does it mean to be a human being?

Let's just start here by agreeing that a human being is a person of possibilities with options that either stem from the highest or lowest potential. It is every human being's choice of potential that determines his/her state of consciousness. It is normal for one to limit himself, and it is also normal for one not to limit himself. You will notice the phrase, "all things are possible..." taken from the greatest mind of creation – Jesus Christ. That phrase embraces the notion that human beings are not supposed to think of themselves lightly in terms of what can come as a result of consciousness. Again, it will be up to each person to acknowledge the kind of outcomes that are to come in his life. There is little that can escape the conception in consciousness of human beings.

Taken from Jesus Christ are the following pieces of infinite awareness of human being potential. "You shall do even greater things than I have done." Does this sound like something that promotes human being? If so, many people that use the term, "I am only human" to embrace imperfection have misarranged the intelligence of being. Reality suggests that human being describes an ongoing process to be whatever you choose—whether that is non achiever or achiever; loser or winner; unintelligent or intelligent; non inventor or inventor; and non believer or believer. The true reality of human being is the role of consciousness and what it identifies. Realistically speaking, everything about human being is identifiable through the conscious. Left to the role of the mystics, this is also referred to as spirit. It is said that the spirit governs that which has been, is, and shall be manifested in the material realm.

It has been my discovery that human being is the reflection of the Infinite Consciousness. It is biblically listed as an offspring of God. This depicts it as a phenomenon. It is not totally understood in terms of what can be possible of it. I suggest that nothing be ruled out of its capability, especially since God is not completely understood.

Having come this far with human being, let's take a quantum leap. The mystics have attempted to define human being before, and no one has gotten past assigning it to the term of man. When asked, "What is man"? The following answer has been given: the image of God. This however, suggests that no one fully knows. What is certain is that human being is a creature of higher knowing and the same applies to God. On the one hand, human being is reality knowledge, free will, and conscious.

What is not known is how its body was tampered together due to the fact that its organs were predetermined in a perfect functioning manner. Today scientists remain fascinated with studying the function of the total human being. My knowledge is that the human being functioning is the system to observe should we want to know more about God and/or Infinite Intelligence. So far, I have not addressed the inquiry of the boundaries of human being. Whereas there are yet things to be discovered about our being, there exist some boundaries. The only boundary that the scientific community has discovered is that human being does not live forever in the physical body.

Beyond the body remains to be a burden of truth, and it has to be dealt with on the accounts of individual beliefs, faith, and choice. The reality of human being means that you choose the kind of life you live. You, therefore, must become accountable for the outcomes in your life. Discovering yourself and awaking to your inner consciousness, which is the giver of every meaning associated with your life, can put you on the path to recovery and success.

I am a human being. I am nothing short of potential and possibility. I am the "I" in all that experience, all conscious phases of the present and future. Equally important, without your conceptualizing yourself as the "I" in human being, creating and erasing meaning present and meaning to come, nothing can be experienced that is or is to come unless the "I" within your being gives it permission.

You are the "I" existing in your being and without being there, your being ceases to exist. The "I" in you is capable of waking up in other realms beyond your body. So what it means to be human being is fully not knowable. To this end, eyes have not seen, neither ears have heard, or even your feelings have identified what you are completely. At best, human being is miraculous.

Human beings discover pure reality via their internal dialogue and/or via the soul.

Reform Your Reality Reform Your Life

10

Subconscious Mind

Reality has always been the finished perception that surfaces in the part of the mind below the level of conscious perception that evolves to give you the alertness needed to bring you from the past to another state of mindfulness. There are moments in your life when you are not wholly conscious to your maximum potential, likely, due to the fallen nature of man—t*he subconscious mind*! If there has ever been a need for you to face it, chances are there were moments when you could have gone ahead of your fears to discover grander realities for yourself which would have probably rendered you desirable outcomes. Well, it is natural to have seen this happen in your life. Chances are that if this ever happened to you, it meant at the time that you were victim to your subconscious mind.

The subconscious mind is not realistic when it comes to cutting - edge vision. Simply, the subconscious mind previews your life in a way that negates *faith*. What is more, it distracts you from evolving mentally into a balanced person. Psychoanalytically speaking, research and statistics do show that the subconscious mind when overwhelmed becomes a tool of destruction. Human being existence during its genesis stage was victimized by the subconscious mind. So many accounts of less than moral activities recorded biblically are the result of it. This follows the notion of the subconscious mind being demonic. "Resist not evil," coined by Jesus Christ, I take to mean "do not fear your subconscious mind."

Instead face it and seek to save it from ruining your life and other lives. I say go, get out of the hand of death! Once you do, you will be able to tame every illusion born, and nothing shall in any wise be able to harm you again. You then become as the conscious of God. The subconscious mind, if not enlightened, is the foundation of inner conflict or mental disorder. It is a type of cancer psychologically to the brain which is the real blame for ruin on the surface level of life. Literally, it is fear. It is the one aspect of human beings that most are afraid to face. Of course, a Soul born has chosen to go inside of it and return to us as Spiritual Leader—Jesus. The function of the subconscious mind is to create illusion because it only processes everything from below and/or less than conscious level of reality. Since I have termed the subconscious mind as demonic, its converted state is the nature of being Godlike.

The Godlike nature comes as a result of converting every less than perfect attitude, perception, and demonic inner motion imaginable. This is the work facing every born soul. For example, from Adam to the last soul born, the subconscious mind had and/or has to be converted to higher

84

consciousness—Godlike—should the human being establish internal peace. If you look closely, every biblical story with an interaction attributed to God has resulted in either a spiritual conversion with a miraculous ending or a supernatural revelation that promoted awareness of higher consciousness, even future things. To be exact, the chosen soul among every culture delved deepest into the realm of the subconscious to bring us to the knowledge of being consciously awakened to psychosis. These chosen persons found throughout the history of the world are revered today as enlightened beings, prophets, spiritual gurus, and awakened souls. I have been victimized somewhat by my subconscious during my weakest moments and before I became an awakened man of God. In those times, my thoughts were below my fullest potential and possibility.

Maybe, you've had a different experience. Nevertheless, the experience of the subconscious mind is far less rewarding than an outcome associated with faith. It has been my personal experience, that faith rescues the subconscious mind by resolving all of its uncertainties with the full assurance of handling any and/or everything mentally challenging to the mind. This is most important about successful fundamentals of reality. Whereas faith dissolves fear that exists subconsciously in the mind, only a shift in consciousness evolves the mind so that it experiences awakening. The process of achieving greater awareness of nature, human being, and even cosmic knowing is the result of a shift in consciousness. Bringing the Divine to the surface is the inward attentive presence of waking awareness perceptible by human being at any given moment. It hands over thought, will, or perception. This waking presence is the offering of Divinity, Spirit of God. Thus, the subconscious mind is replaced by a heightened awareness. Reality from the perspective of higher consciousness suggests that one comes above his subconscious to an awakened Godlike intelligence to erect abundant outcomes and futuristic manifestations associated with his life.

The goal of consciousness is to strive to master the subconscious mind rather than its being able to tame your mind from reaching ultimate states of reality. If you are attentive to your divinity, you will experience life as being resurrected from the dead in mental a capacity. Higher consciousness is the prize of inner peace or a peace that surpasses the subconscious mind. What I have noticed about myself is those changes took place in my imagination. For me, there arose new and improved conceptualizations. Inspired by higher consciousness (Holy Spirit), it releases supernatural intelligence to develop your conscious. Upon its arrival, there come abundant revelations of things that are unborn; things that escaped the vision of the eye; and fusions of restored motions of bliss. In the awakened conscious, one experiences keen alertness of both distant and present things. To illustrate, a knowing is born that encompasses insightfulness of the nature of the soul; the nature of the cosmic soul; and also, the characteristics and nature of animals.

The realization of the development of consciousness is anchored by the nature of vibrations of God within the human being. This suggests that vibrations of space, divinity, and distant time reside some place within human being make up. This is to say, that transforming the subconscious mind is very much the possibility of every soul; and to disbelieve that existence of inward intuitive realization might very well set back the process of the human being's subconscious from escape of the ruin it's capable of causing in every aspect of creation.

Consciousness in the mind creates meaning for all that was, is, shall be, and everlastingly to appear. Also it's the tool to replace the subconscious mind with realization. Things lost to memory and detachment are assigned to higher consciousness. The human being and its

its possession of higher consciousness is yet
to be defined.

> **T**he subconscious mind
> is to be taken into your
> internal dialogue for it
> to face reality.

11

Perception

Nothing in life has been so much a determining factor as your perception about things happening in your life or not happening in your life. Somehow, later in your life rather than earlier in your life, it is easy to allow your mind to govern your direction in life; therefore, you tend to recognize it as sacred, thus, walking in the path that it has outlined. This is the way just about every person on the planet functions. Seemingly, it's a good method until something goes wrong. For the most part, it works okay for everyone that lives this way. All people experience this basic way of interpreting their lives for a while. This is the perception of people that apply everything to a mental impression being the basic component in the formation of perception.

With this being said, many people will agree that a mental concept of a piece of data applies to what is capable of being interpreted with the mind and, therefore, the sum being their perception. By now, it would probably seem indifferent or self afflicting not to pattern your life and/or its direction after your perception because you now have a habit of viewing your life from this perspective. Likely, everything about your life is perceived on thoughts in your mind or thoughts entering your mind. To you, your mental outlook is always internalizing and/or giving meaning to everything in life. Your perception is the giver of meaning in your life at first since it is the result of the neurological process by which such recognition and interpretation of your life are affected.

This fundamental of reality can serve you adequately for seasons during your life, but at a certain time in your life, the truth is that it's a fragile reality; therefore, it has to be overcome should there be for you an awakening to infinite reality. On the one hand, perception is connected to your sensory; likely, the sense of sight. Your eyes support your mind. On the other hand, perception is not Infinite reality. Infinite reality goes beyond sensory delight; thus, it does not depend on the psychological chemistry of your mind. Infinite reality does take your mind across seemingly the vast neurological ocean of your thoughts to connect you to the infinite world of *faith and hope.* Whereas the essence of perception pacifies your sense of sight, overcoming your sense of sight introduces you to the realm of absolute freedom of your mind.

You no longer need to depend on it because it becomes subject to your new born spirituality—being *faith* and *hope.* To compare your mind to the potentiality of faith or hope, you would have to surrender your thoughts perception!

In a very real way, surrendering your mind to the audacity of faith is the same as making your mind confident that it needs no perception going forward with your life. *Faith* and *hope* behave mysteriously, and they are the only two phenomena that can pick up your mind when it gives up. Have you ever wondered what will happen to your perception if you ever get to the point in your life where you accept both the best and worst about what you are to face at a certain moment that you have to confront?

Your perception collapses to a freedom that you no longer need your mind to confirm you one way or the other. This is the type of freedom that comes to rescue your mind—perception—from what you fear and by what you are being challenged. One of the main reasons that perception is fragile reality is because it is a product of your mind. Equally significant is the fact that your mind can only function and/or work by thoughts. Otherwise, it has nothing to govern it. Here is an example. If you are facing a challenge of which you have no knowledge, how can your mind provide you a perception that can solve that which it has no knowledge to project? It can't. It won't; therefore, it becomes often fragile reality to totally depend on your perception for the duration of your life. Perception is walking according to your mind whereas faith is not walking by sight and thus, a type of reality distant of the mind.

Any mind that projects perception of temporal things will never be free to experience those things which manifest into the world independent of reason. Though perception can be fragile at times, it causes one to exclude himself from further reaches of consciousness; yet infinite reality looks not on the things which are perceptible, instead, those things which are manifested by the mystery of *faith* and/or *hope*. The fragility of perception is that it stands on changing points of view. Often, one comes after the other as the mind embraces new meaning frequently. Thus, what ends up happening for the duration of the life of one totally depending on his perception is he becomes a stockpile of realities.

The goal to be achieved for all life is ultimate reality and infinite consciousness to rebound from fragile perception's rising and falling. Thus, let faith and hope inspire your eyes to discover the miraculous awakening to an infinite reality, a journey that will not require them to behave by sight—perception. Although your eyes are the light of your body, they can only take you so far. Although perception is the projection associated with your eyes, in many cases, the visibility and/or invisibility of some things do not always determine a definite outcome. To illustrate, you have no way of knowing for certain how outcomes will turn out that have not completed its process; therefore, perception about unfolding manifestation must not be left in the possession of the eye.

Instead, cultivating your inner self with an awareness beyond perception is most rewarding to you. Such awareness to be achieved is that of non - judgment awareness when it comes to outcomes that you expect to materialize in your life. Let not your assessment about much of everything be consumed by the visibility of your perception. Should your eyes ever forecast defeat and/or an end, just know that you can begin to envision beyond such perception if you erase your initial judgment. Non judgment is a type of eraser of meaning; thus, it's an instrument to be used to induce peace. In my life, I can truly say that most times when I have projected the worst, it has turned out to be the best outcome to happen for me at that time in my life. Does this sound familiar to you?

I am sure both of us could tell long stories about countless situations in which we've been. What is certain about outcomes that we often project and/or give meaning, is that things do not appear what they can be. Perception, then in most cases is a fragile reality! It is wise not to place yourself in perception: on the one hand, personally and on the other hand, into the matrix of other's lives. I am sure that you can identify with that insight! Another way to view perception is to accept that it is sight based! The words of Jesus Christ "The light of the body is the eye." To add a thought, it rewards you if you understand that you are to be careful and responsible how you allow things to light up before your eyes. Perception includes how you agree to give meaning to things that come to light.

Watch it closely to correct it if it offends your vitality and/or well being. For example, if your perception is judgmental in any way at all, chances are that your entire outlook will be reflective of your perception. Equally important, your point of view about anything embraces your perception. Most helpful is lack of perception about most things. Judge not most things and you will be at peace. Judgment creates meaning which is perception, and non judgment erases it. The meaning of life is yet to be fully determined, but I say perception cannot reveal it alone.

Perception is re-formed by re-formed reality.

Never underestimate the power entrusted to reformed reality. The power of your internal dialogue is entrusted with infinite wisdom, awareness, and reality. As an intellectual being, certain capabilities are given to you that were not given to other species; therefore, they were entrusted to your internal dialogue with self and the reality of God.

Reform Your Reality Reform Your Life

12

Ordinary Reality

As a general rule, the acquiring of knowledge through learned behavior, typically an instructed morality usually in the common manner, is seen as ordinary reality. At some point in everyone's life, all of us from children have experienced identifying all that we understood to be educational when it came to grasping ordinary things. It was and always will be for me ordinary reality to the extent that it offered me ordinary truth. Living in a world that is so complex and vastly different from all that you learn as a child growing up, especially giving rise to all those imaginary things that you were instructed to believe, comes to full circle when you are faced with the real world. Your having to identify with a different reality other than what you were accustomed seems to demand so much more than the reality commonly encountered during your innocence.

Ordinary reality is a beginning reality. Once you launch out into the real world where laws legislate morality, you become accountable to a system rather than your parent's rules. For this reason, life requires an exceptional knowledge about how to interpret all of its rules. Sometimes the rules are ordinary and other times the rules are not so ordinary. There will be times that you are expected to understand courses of events with an above ordinary degree of reality. In such instances, most, if not a great deal of your freedom, depends on it. For example, the judicial system is a great illustration.

Reality is birthed in the internal dialogue. Re-form your reality; Re-form your life.

Refusal of having above average reality to direct your conduct in the public might land you a night in a jail cell and countless other setbacks should your ordinary reality be in conflict with the law. The purpose of ordinary reality is for you to experience the following: First, recognize yourself and others; second, there are consequences for your actions. They are always good or bad, but they require that you encounter specific outcomes. Last, identify with life and how to be identified. At best, you are to make the best of what was handed down to you for you to accept and/or believe with an emphasis on respect for others. For me, ordinary reality has been my beginner course for life.

The wisdom of Apostle Paul, an apostle of Jesus Christ is emblematic of what I have termed ordinary reality, "When I was a child, I spake as a child, I understood as a child, I thought as a child: but when I became a man (mature), I put away childish things." What I have learned about myself is that during my youth, I was given, at best, part of the whole reality instead of perfect reality. It's the way that most people understood it after they matured says Paul. I came to the discovery that as my life evolved, I required more and more of an ultimate and/or perfect reality. This notion can be tricky because you only require the reality for your present maturity, so you were told. Like I was told, you can't handle all of it at one time. Truthfully, I wanted to make that decision for myself, but as it was, I was just a child or little boy being too inquisitive. One thing that I've believed always is when perfect awareness arrives, partial knowing disappears.

I don't really conclude my curiosity for wanting a perfect awareness at an early time in my life to be good or bad. I just was born with that determination. Ordinary reality manifests itself in every aspect of your communication like anything else that is within you. Starting with your words, ordinary reality is reflected. Your words are the reflection of your identity. At the utterance of every word is the thought that fashions it. Next, your understanding is fashioned after your inner identification. What you will discover at any degree of reality is that it's your own thinking. Ordinary reality profits much when you are a youth; however, as you age, much more understanding is required of you.

At some part of your life, making ordinary reality a priority suggests that it gives place to new reality. Nothing stays the same forever on the physical surface. Only eternal things remain the same, and therefore, the things unseen and/or born belong not to reality. Instead, those eternal things belong outside of meaning because they are vibrations of possibility and potentiality.

Altered reality isn't commonly accepted among people. Much like ordinary reality, you tend to trap yourself into what you are instructed to believe, accept, and hold to be true. I've seen so many people perish by lack of understanding the purpose of an altered reality. The definition of an altered reality is summed by one word, change! Although, in a world where everything is arriving and departing, coming and going, beginning and ending, and starting and finishing, people do not embrace change, the reason for so much misfortune in all of our lives. *Observing mistakes in consciousness is the premise of an altered reality.* Changing your reality is a must if it makes things better for you and all others around you. Nothing is unfruitful about being different. Since reality is fragile because of its expiration with time, reality alters when you can identify with things deeper. It is profitable always to embrace flexibility when it comes to your reality. It ensures that your emotions and feelings are kept from injury or damage. A flexible reality is to maintain an open mind. Consequently, those persons unwilling to embrace adjustability usually are restricted to one reality about everything. Mostly, their first reality is likely their lasting reality. Sometimes, people with restricting reality forget to grow and therefore, impede an altered reality.

Reality in every way possible should be adaptable to higher consciousness. While society can pose a burden if not interpreted with understanding and the position of your inner self in it, disorder can destabilize even the basic identification of life. Furthermore, resistance to heightened reality can set back outcomes associated with promotion. An altered reality is centered around possibility. The fact that things occur without anyone's input and therefore, as things happen, the best position to embrace is adaptability. When you can do this, potential for favorable outcomes will be the result. Living in a society where laws, rules, and circumstances are never permanent, clinging to an altered reality and/or an open mind produces the best character always.

Just think about how many times refusal on your behalf of having an adjustable reality has caused you setbacks. Not having an altered reality when you need to have it, keeps you from moving ahead with your life.

It is always better to let go rather

than hold on to a reality that impacts you negatively. For instance, so many people use the statement "learn from your mistakes." This all the more reinforces the need to welcome into your mind the notion that reality takes on changes. What is more, having an altered experience suggests that you are willing to grow. So many times growth has been postponed because of stationary reality.

What I have discovered about myself is that I am a better person when I have come through some experience and gained a higher understanding as of result of having gone through it. You, too, are likely to experience the same. Each time that I have overcome a challenge in my life, it has always altered my reality. Mostly, it has left me with a grander self awareness rather than anything else. Just about every time I had an altered reality, it's because of self—actualizing moments, even higher vibrations of consciousness. At anytime higher consciousness is being experienced, reality is being altered to some degree. Higher consciousness comes to redesign reality and thus, alter the identification of it. For this reason alone, altered reality is better than ordinary reality. It has always been the focus of progressive minded people to want extraordinary outcomes.

With the manifestation of extraordinary outcomes, comes also an extraordinary consciousness. Altered vibrations in your mind field are the result of expanding consciousness. The more conscious expands, the more likely you are to encounter altered reality. All things pertaining to the internal world and external world involve some notion of reality. Equally significant, identification of possibility, potentiality, and reality adjustments is the work of consciousness. If you ever want to be serious about monitoring activity that calculates supernatural outcomes in your life, just know that outcomes are manifested according to your reality of the world.

> Change your reality
> and reality changes
> your life.

Often, altered reality takes place to transition you from one level of identification to another level. Much is true about transition reality. More reality is the basic formation for heightened consciousness to transform the mind's position in its field. The mind is an abstract frequency in the brain that vibrates on the basis of consciousness. It transfers mental energy, visual energy, and specks of miraculous energy. Only this field of consciousness is responsible for transforming reality from one position to another position in the mind. Transition reality starts with consciousness. Certainly, conception in consciousness is the component to real transformation in your life.

The conception relative to mental changes occurring in the human being field of consciousness is the transit of new reality. Thus, the nature of your reality markedly changes its appearance or form via your expression. What is more, your values are converted and replaced with a different meaning than previously. What I have discovered about conception's taking place in my mind is that while it takes me over to the infinite frequencies across the known realm so that I get to reality unborn to obtain the goods from the eternal realm, it is resurrecting me from the mental death of unreality. Conception in the mind is a spiritual exercise. All people have them.

Noted in an ancient book written to the Romans, the prolific scholar Apostle Paul penned the words, "Be transformed by the renewing of your mind, that you may prove what is good, and acceptable, and perfect will of God."

There can be no mistakes here for sure in that this truth has survived the ages and today revered as holy among more than half the people on the planet. Reality is transitional but from the form of mental transformational thoughts occurring in consciousness. I go so far as to say that transitional reality is the cure of the mind needed more so than pills even at this time in the history of the world, though, I am not suggesting that medication be discredited. It can buy time for a person until the transition happens. The goal of cure for people and mental illness is more awareness of transitional reality rather than a life time on drugs. Time and time again, the world has seen untreated mental disorder bring people to ruin, from riches to death, especially in the entertainment community.

Whenever the core problem of an issue is treated without the correct therapy, the problem does not go away; rather it keeps coming back for treatment. Increasingly, people are right back to craving what they need most because they overlook it when conditions were met with improper treatment. The world is craving perfect reality. It has been since the fall of man. There have been many sons of God to bring us to that perfect reality but as always very few receive it. Apostle Paul's theory is deeper than preachers teach and preach it. What is meant by renewing your mind with God is that you let it prove the reality of God—good and acceptable and perfect. This is what I say is meant by the will—Reality of God!

As for devotees of Christ, as was the Apostle Paul, their mind and reality were transmissible in consciousness to the Christ Reality, thus, one that claimed to be God's voice. Transition reality has some basic analysis, if understood and can prove, to be one of the best experiences among many to be had. If you allow it to have its perfect work, even the frequency of infinite possibility and potentiality will manifest within you in a material world. Your characteristics will take on new form after transitional reality is finished. What I have discovered for myself is that transitional reality erases mistakes in my perception having occurred over time due to low frequencies in the mind. The finished work of transitional reality is a miracle. You become a miracle, and you gather a new attitude to go with your new reality.

To put it simply, you can return to your life guided by new consciousness, awakened from unreality, and cut off from your previous mistakes having passed over them. In order to see yourself transitioned and triumphant as you move your life ahead, there needs to be a period in your life   for   observation   reality.

Observation reality is the key to evaluating the fundamentals of reality. It is very important not to forget to take time to observe all things including yourself with your life. One evening my friend and I were playing a game of Chinese checkers. She introduced me to the game. Oh, could she play it. It had been taught to her by her mother as a little girl. Very few times I could beat her though I did some. Finally, I said to her after three rounds of being defeated, "What is the gist of this damn game?"

I will agree that I was somewhat ashamed that I was not able to win more times than she did. She said to me, "You are making the game harder than it really is because you are so smart and you what to create for yourself a method to win rather to observe every move." She finally told me, each move is important to the next move, and every move depends on the next move that you need to make to get your marbles to the other side of the board before I do."

I said to her, "You know my problem with the game but you do not want to tell me in order that you keep the edge. Isn't that how the game works?"

She said, "I don't know."

I eventually said, "Tell me what my problem is. You introduced me to this game, and I don't think it to be fair that I should even play without knowing as much as you do about the rules."

In the end, she said to me, "Your problem is that you don't know how to strategize your moves in your mind before you put them into action."

It hit me like a blow; knocked the wind out of me! My reply was, "Thank you" You have awakened me to what I need to have in order to live the last half of my life. I have lived all my life following an intuitive passion as a guide for righteousness concerning things hoped and not seen."

She said, "I know, but I have not felt safe doing it."

I said, "It's a gift to me called faith." Today, I practice both my faith and strategizing moves in my mind before putting them to action. This was a valuable lesson about observation reality. I had to see that observing every move before putting it into action is the game of life, too. When it comes to observation reality, the goal is to become aware.

An awareness of yourself and everything else helps you to see all things for what they can be. Through careful and direct attention, you will notice and/or identify the smallest to the largest things in your life. Reality has a way of presenting itself through observing. One that observes all things usually detects a kind of reality about things truthfully. An observer of the self generally sees the missing reality needed to complete the self. In addition, things such as growth, strength, and weakness, proactive planning and decision making, conformity and non-conformity and knowing are all achieved by getting an eyeful of reality. Lack of paying close attention to obstacles most times shows unreality; therefore, so many things could go wrong for you! All kinds of mistakes usually follow unreality.

The worst being that you forfeit your future and/or your life. You can turn unreality around should you pay attention to the truth about yourself and everything else. The purpose for observing all things is that you be not blinded to its nature. This can keep you away from setbacks and unwanted experiences in your life. So many advancements come by way of noticing how things really work. For example, job promotions in the secular arena are subject to those employees who know how things run efficiently and effectively. The same principle applies when it comes to reality. It's a type of universal principle applied in every form of organization and/or organized effort to establish uniformity among people. I have heard the saying, "be careful" so many times. I learned some time ago that what is really to be implied from the notion is that I observe carefully all things along the way. I am sure that you have been given the same advice. With that being said, you now have an interpretation of what I termed to be observation reality. To apply this advice daily come, you may escape pitfalls that could impede your progress as you are going through life. Diligent observation is the secret to uncovering reality. It is said that if you observe things long enough, you can find anything for which you are searching. Lessons in every aspect of life are obtained by coming in contact with observation. Illustrative of this notion is a classroom setting of an instructor and students. Just about every instructor and every student alike will agree that getting an understanding of the nature of what is being discussed largely comes by observation of instructions.

Learning to observe is a proactive measure taken on your behalf that rewards you every step of the way as you move through the abstract field of your mind in consciousness, discovering the hidden things rarely noticed and bringing forth the dawning of your mentally resurrected self. Observation reality is a channel in frequency that conveys just about all that was and is and is to come. What a good outcome! That's what I say. Nothing can escape diligence. No not even the perfect reality. Mystical reality being God reality is the last of the fundamentals of reality. It's the final reality discovered and experienced among human beings. So much about it is not embraced because God is the abstract Spirit within every aspect of creation, even you and me.

Only because spirit is abstract in the mind residing in the field of our conscious, it has to be explained differently from reason and/or logic as many would have it. Thus, it's the reason some can't fathom the notion of God. On the other hand, many choose to identify with God reality via inspiration which comes out from the mind as an abstract spirit to the brain that vibrates consciousness. Such reality holds the secrets of the universe: wisdom and revelation, awareness and insightfulness, understanding and prudence, the beginning and the ending, and origin the creation. The reality of God is the Spirit of God! It's the most intellectually challenged realism because this reality isn't found by material instruments used in the scientific community or measured by time.

Therefore, its measure is longer than the earth and broader than the sea, only imaginable by abstract spirit/reality itself. On another hand, the mystical reality is revealed. The best way to interpret it is by inception and conception which take place within consciousness to release absolute inspiration that gives understanding. The reality of God is that the Spirit of God is the make-up of consciousness and thus, a real entity. Without it, no life can exist. In a very real sense, rather than needing to design a mental image of God, wisdom would have you accept God for what God is instead of personalizing God with an image. Realistically the truth is all people who attempt to discredit God do so because they have not been willing to accept what they cannot change about themselves and their loved ones when events happen beyond their control.

As opinion would have it, some might not like or accept the reality of God, but this does not mean it ceases to exist. What does exist is the need to understand God. It has been the curiosity of every generation to know God personally.

I believe it to be okay just to know God intuitively. Personal things have a sort of biased perspective and in the long haul are subject to favoritism. Surely, this kind of reality would not fit the description of God. The real question each generation asks itself is two-fold: Is there a perfect reality and if so, can God be found to give it? Surely, many people have tried to understand this phenomenon, especially during moments of grief, terminal illness, catastrophe, and unanswered questions.

God is the Spirit and
reality which birth
your internal dialogue.

Human beings are incomplete of an

all encompassing peace until their possession of the internal dialogue awakens within themselves and begins to reason with self about what is truth and everlasting. Some identify the dialogue as communication with God, and others embrace it as the inner self—*Soul*. All and all both schools of thought are acceptable in that both are akin and inseparable. Human beings can go for days even years in their lives not facing reality until they run into barricades and/or come to a place mentally where they envision the need of assistance of the highest power in order that a new outcome happens.

At this point, most of us observe a glimpse of the reality of God's being real for us. Therefore, an internal dialogue with reality is the initial path to lasting peace with God. An exceptional life with God begins with a dialogue with yourself and reality to include the abstract Spirit Mediator–God–to assure you of peace when necessary. Also, God assures you of hope, friendship, companionship, and the voice of reasoning in the internal dialogue. God is thus, interpreted as Higher Consciousness, Ultimate Reality, and Spirit. Key to the reality of God is the opportunity for you to express yourself, explain yourself, and petition for yourself without any interruption or rejection. The reality of the internal dialogue is typical of a meeting place for you and God to exchange.

Comparing it to paradise is acceptable because you bring your all to God. Nothing can be more rewarding in life than that. All those having experienced the calm from establishing an internal dialogue agree that it provides you an opportunity to release any unwanted perception which previously occurred during your life while at the same time it hands down new awareness. Most important, it provides a type of exit away from unwanted memory. It's a renewal reality that is born from facing internal reality and accepting it as mystical reality. Overall, samples of the best possible reality, being the foundation on which you reform your life, should be self-actualizing reality. Mystical reality, therefore, is entrusted to us through meditation and after praying.

Praying and meditation are expressions happening within one's internal dialogue, from which reality originates. It would be a mistake not to take seriously the impact of reality that is discovered from praying and meditation.

Unless you emphasize all that can be self enhancing when it comes to higher consciousness, mystical reality is misunderstood. You will either know all there is to know or not about ways which lead to self improvement. All that can be most rewarding to you about mystical reality is explored when you commune with yourself and the reality of God in an internal dialogue. By so doing, you are able to interact with higher consciousness, deeper insights about infinite reality and insurmountable awareness.

During your discovery of reality stemming from your internal dialogue, the soul releases sincere truth pertaining to the best outcome for you to obtain wholesomeness. What is more, your internal dialogue communicates a heightened consciousness that expresses itself in such a way that nothing can be misunderstood. What I have found out about myself is that through communicating my concerns about all things pertaining to me and the reality of God during an internal dialogue, my reality becomes purer and therefore, my reality changes from basic tendencies to advanced tendencies.

> **M**ystical reality is all
> about the dialogue occurring
> within you about yourself
> and the reality of God!

People have always exchanged dialogue within themselves hoping that it's being received in a mystical sphere in order that they would collect an abundance of revelation with which to empower themselves and the world in which they live, including other people, places and things. From experience, I have benefitted greatly from my daily interpersonal dialogue. All the intention of my interpersonal dialogue has been to bring me to escalated consciousness, so that I am able to interact with life exhibiting my best potential. Nothing is so fulfilling as the assurance coming from an internal dialogue from which reality comes. To ensure yourself of inner peace, mystical reality allows you to experience beyond what you have been able to experience in your life.

The ultimate purpose of mystical reality is to sustain your spirit from all that may wound it and therefore, to provide you advanced direction daily.

Lastly, establishing the life of peacefulness rewards you best as you practice daily structuring your interpersonal dialogue with all things to be examined. As you interact more with mystical reality, you will discover what always appears true about yourself and others. There is no other instructor like your internal dialogue to teach you truth, prepare you for readiness to deal with life, and give you genuine peace and freedom. All in all, mystical reality transmits perfect reality.

Part II

Re-form Your Reality
"Re-form Your Life"

Reform Your Reality Reform Your Life

13

See Problems Not As Protests but Needing Solutions

Reforming your reality is the key to reforming your life. It's the very necessary part of your existence that plays the role of identifying your life. To begin, reform should start with reality and, therefore, identifying your life from the best pattern of perception. I would suggest that it is best for you to see how improvement and correction can be presented coming out from the worst imaginable problem having occurred in your life. All problems are not bad challenges; instead, all that grievance suggests is that you need to come up with a solution of reform. In a very germane way, reform is the process of formulating results and/or outcomes differently.

This process works in any area of your life; thus, you can redo, remake, and reposition yourself holistically. I have learned to reform my life by reforming my reality about what happens in my life. You can do the same. What I have discovered about myself is that when I choose not to see problems in my life and/or differences of opinion between myself and someone else, I tend to be sensitive to the notion that a solution is being demanded, not just any solution but the best possible solution to benefit all parties involved. In most cases where you meet difficulty in your life, you are being asked to take on the personal role of being the reformer of the situation. What is more, a majority of people not willing to reform themselves in a crisis usually experience major, if not life-defeating setbacks.

There is one reason for not bringing the best possible solution to any problem that you might face—too lazy to think of one! Chances are that it is not as easy as it sounds. Thinking of solutions requires deep thought, meditation, reasoning, and wisdom. Many people who are lazy want other people to do for them what they won't do for themselves. Bringing into your life reform and meaningful solutions to dissolve your un-readiness about so-called protests that you are facing is only a matter of choosing your thoughts, making choices, and using energy pragmatically. The process is not quick, but it takes some time to do it efficiently. If patience is missing from the equation of coining solutions, there won't be one to come. The result then, is always stagnation and/or complacency.

Reforming your reality rids you of complacency. It turns all things around in your life and the lives in which you are involved. Usually, it makes better all lives. Making the choice to reform your life is among the best things that you can do for yourself.

It is the type of rectification that only you can do for yourself superseding anyone else's doing it for you.

Reforming your life is
the result of advancing
your life in all the ways
seemingly good for you.

It's most rewarding! Take some time out today and begin to observe yourself reborn including everything that you would want to be. Next take the initiative to have the audacity to believe that you can be reformed should you choose to formulate your mind different from your previous thinking.

Last, take the journey in consciousness to revolutionize your reality with an emphasis on reforming your life. Use every fundamental of reality as a guide to remaking yourself internally so that you have a keen sense of awareness of yourself as you journey along. Live your life with passion to reform it from day to day. Reforming yourself is keeping you timeless and ageless internally. You can also reform your brains as your reform your reality. Nothing new about it! Just remember that you are never too young or too old to reform.

Contrary to the logic of many, I do not agree that human beings get too old or too young to learn. It's just a matter of being inspired by the right reason to change. Isn't that true? Whenever I admire someone, beauty and appreciation stand out because of my attitude of acceptance. I see their adaptability to being relevant to the times. To me, that reforms.

If you are ever going to be the best that you can be, making yourself over is not so bad. Please understand that I am not asking you to change your career or spouse, rather revisit how you interact with them in order to keep life interesting. Coming full circle with your life is learning to position yourself in order to reform your reality, thus reforming your life.

Reform Your Reality Reform Your Life

14

Live Objectively Rather Than Subjectively

The life that is likely to experience abundant freedoms and happiness holistically often is the life having been objective rather than subjective to social pressures, opinions of others, and religious dogma. Being objective about your life is having actual existence of reality uninfluenced by emotions or personal prejudices. Whatever your passion in life, pursue it! Do so without the distraction of other people's opinion about it. By all means, weigh any insight to be helpful to your passion, but do not change your passion. Instead build on your passion. The very passion in your heart is interconnected to your destiny. I have seen too many people live their lives to appease others and never really come into their own.

These people are really ever happy, and rarely do they live healthy productive lives because they have suppressed the very life intended for them. Most times they overlook the vast freedoms of human being. Usually outside influences tame the will to be independent. Thus, they live statistical lives predicted by cultural norms and hardly ever experience abundance according to their potential. In order to reform your life holistically, you will need to break away from institutionalized reality. Because you live and strive in an atmosphere where everything is constantly changing, you also have to be constant in changing your reality to accommodate your expected goal. Detouring from being subjective to the prediction of others is in itself a type of cutting-edge reality.

It allows you to be free to be new. As you open yourself to the newness of your potential and possibilities, so come new thoughts, new ideals, new courage, new energy, and new ambitions. All of which are the answers to setting yourself apart from the status quo culture. By so doing, you give yourself opportunity to participate in the options for your life. It is necessary that you allow your choices to be free and independent of the options someone else prescribed for your life. Whenever you make yourself subject to any mind other than your own, you are allowing someone else to think for you about what you can or cannot do. It is best for the world that *you* contribute your own individuality so that the world has to offer more.

Many successful people would agree that freedom to be what you feel passionate about being in your life leads to a more meaningful and productive life. Giving yourself an opportunity to do something new might very well prove that you hold the next invention in the world in your passion and possession. Wow! What an invention the world could suffer should you not have the assurance of being confident while being different from most people on the planet. Just about 90 percent of the people on the planet are afraid to live freely because they've had their minds locked outside of individuality while depending on society to hold their future in its plans for their lives. I have lived opposite of this reality all my life ever since I can remember. In my life, I have done mostly all things to contribute to the self worth of other people.

It was 39 years later that I realized that I needed to do things with the same heart but with a different priority. This suggested making myself satisfied; then, if I am able to share with others that want to receive of it, do so. Since then, I have reformed my reality which also reformed my life. The sooner you take control of your life the faster lasting happiness and freedoms come to it. Reforming your life is reforming your reality from fear associated with being free from the social customs and traditions of your life time. When you are opened minded to experience your own creative passion, you are objective rather than subjective and you, therefore, change the path of prediction for your life.

Too many times if you've ever allowed yourself to be subjected to any passion other than your own, you have had to suppress your coming forth in a way unbecoming of your creativity. To do so, is to delay your individual passion. The best life is lived by passion. It's as if you are doing everything with a type of effortless willingness. This makes life happy! Thus, your life takes on a meaning consistent with your destiny. Reform your life by reforming the reality which suggests to you that you ought to be subjected to a particular path in your life. Make sure that your ambition is yours not others. If you do so, you will find that whereas you have regretted not giving or doing all that you could have, that doing all that you could have leaves no regrets in your heart no matter the outcome. It is likely that you will not condemn yourself ever again for any reason. Chances are that you won't ever have a reason when you live objectively instead of subjectively.

Reforming your life is not as easy as you want it to be, but it makes

inner peace easier to obtain.

To some degree, conditioning yourself to be free to be objective makes your life worth living. At least, this has been my experience with life. Carrying out your passionate obligation to be the best that you can be is a type of self awakening. In the process of awakening to your real passion, always remember to reform every aspect of yourself to include bearing all and enduring all that you need to come into your own creative self.

15

Be Comfortable Standing Alone

The position in life most rejected is the courage to stand alone. Only about ten percent of the people on planet earth are comfortable standing alone. Being comfortable standing alone seems to be the talk many have assigned to God until it is time for honors to be acknowledged. In a very real way, reforming your reality can sometimes seem like you have to stand alone. It is most difficult to do because you have been taught to love and have respect for being accepted or just fitting in with everyone and everything in your life. Greatness is not achieved in unison although team work is remarkable. There are times in your life that you need to go after your dreams and passions alone. You will encounter during your pursuit to greatness times when you lose touch with people that you want to be with you all the way to the finishing point of your achievement.

What I have discovered about my own accomplishments is that people are with you sometimes, not all the time. The lesson of the victor is that victory comes to you in personal form before it can come to all those persons whom it needs to include. When the term alone is used in most contexts, people usually envision conditions of isolation, abandonment, lonesomeness, and being companionless. What I am addressing as being comfortable alone is so much more than the above - mentioned. This is really never the reality for victors. To go ahead instead is to be comfortable alone. Most leaders have figured this out; therefore, you have reverenced them to be the leaders they are in life. Being able to go ahead of the fears, misconceptions, and limits of others is exactly what it means to be comfortable alone.

In the grand scheme of it all, it is most rewarding to reform how you define going after things alone. In the ecumenical community, comfortable being alone simply means, "I will go if I have to go by myself."

Moving ahead sometimes

requires that you move
alone.

This is to be interpreted as unique.
Should you someday really master reform in
your life, it will be because you are serious
about not fearing being matchless and
incomparable. The truth is that all of the
greatest thinkers of all times were
comfortable being alone.

It is the price that you have to pay to
stand out among others. If you are never
comfortable alone, you can never exceed
the standard established before you; thus,
you, to some degree, will never move your
life ahead. This can be applied to your life
even if you don't want it to proposition you.
It usually comes in the form of do or die
situations! When it happens to any one,
usually it happens at the time that is

unwanted. Just think about it, all of the heroes that have mentally shaped the world and, for the most part those who have shaped our reality, are people who moved ahead of the barriers during their life time to discover greatness for the rest of the world no matter the price they had to pay. They were peerless! Solely, they were comfortable alone. One ancient practice that reinforced this notion was and still is meditation!

Until you are able to reform yourself from the fears of being alone in what you choose to do and say, you impede your own progress to greatness. Had it not been for people like Jesus, Who willingly embraced grief, sorrow, rejection, scorn, and beatings, I might not have ever found the answers to salvation. There are other spiritual leaders, politicians, statesmen, celebrities, teachers, parents, and human beings that fit the framework of being comfortable alone. For me, I have had to embrace being comfortable alone in order to do many of things that I am doing today. Leaders are defined by being comfortable alone, and followers are, too! You can tell the difference. Which are you? Life has a subtle way of presenting you before the world without your permission; however, you do have an input on what the world can see of you.

Let yourself do things that you want to do, things you have been afraid to do, even if you have to go at it alone. Get use to it! Whenever it is this way for you, something great wants to present itself to you. Don't fear it! Embrace it! Your life is filled with wonder that you have aborted. It's time for you to reposition your reality and reform your life for the wonder that you've left behind. The greater the challenge the greater the pleasure when it has been endured. There are times that you need to be comfortable alone for your children, for the community, for your passion and purpose! It is time for you to cut off fear of being alone if you want to be great in your short life. All the ways of being denied the abundance of recognition and being long lived have been that you have not been willing to embrace being comfortable alone.

There are some victories that only you are worthy to accomplish and it is time for you to accept your uniqueness. With your faith and prayers, no task is too hard for you, even going ahead of all those people who are afraid to do what you are about to do and those that failed along their way doing what only you are called to do. You were born to do what others cannot do! Reform your life today. Take the road less traveled if you must and know that you will never be forgotten because you trusted to dare fear of being comfortable alone!

My life has changed drastically because I have disassociated it from fear of being comfortable alone. I remind myself when I need to that I am not alone; instead, I am unique. The journey that you are on often sends you into new territories so that you may obtain new victories. You were never designed to be complacent to greatness! There is an "I am" in you screaming to be free to experience victories to come and joy unborn; Release it and let it be free being comfortable alone.

"I am with you always."---Jesus Christ!

Reform your life to
accommodate being unique,
even unequalled!

There is a new thing to be done by
your hands as you see yourself going ahead
of your fear of being alone to achieve it.

Reform Your Reality Reform Your Life

16

Depend on Your Own Experiences to Form Opinions and Views

You will be met by various opinions wanted and unwanted during your lifetime. Some are true and others not true. There will be things that work good for some people in their lives and not work best in the lives of others. The best opinion to rely on is none. Your life is best formed by your own experiences. That which works for some may not work for others. So many things depend on timing, conditions, and individuals. Wisdom suggests that you adhere to your happenings. Many in which you've already been involved can best serve you when you have choices to make and roads to take. Nothing can assure you like your very own experiences. Reforming your life is the notion of listening to your own mind.

Your mind extrapolates the wisdom of your experiences.

From this known range, you will best form your ideals based upon what you know from experience. Let your action reflect where you have been and what you have discovered, never what you have heard and/or that which you have been told. Expect your experiences to lead you away from other people's persuasions. Wait for your learned wisdom to assist you always no matter the temptation to concede to the pitch of others. Let your mind retrieve for you the clarity which you have attained from experience. Reserve your input until you know what to do about life based on the instructions you've gotten from your participation with life.

All that you have encountered is there to instruct you. Reality that reforms your life is self experienced. Too many times, all of us have been victim to handed down prejudices and persuasions with which to establish values. Many of which if you were to examine closely, you would agree that such views are expired and no longer considered to be relevant. Live by governing your reality according to what is acceptable with regard to the time at hand. Certainly this will prove to keep your values in front instead of behind understanding when considering what you ought to do. It is important for you to ask yourself if you believe that people change their minds from time to time. Also, they change their view at the same time. Much of the progress of the future is due to expired reality; thus, reformed reality is the push of the future.

With this being said, it will be best for all people to listen to their own hearts rather than someone else's to establish values and views. Living in a society where the majority dictates the policy with which to govern its people, people are notorious in their persuasion to influence your minds so that they subtlety tame your independent thinking. Growing up as a child, I was always told to let my conscience be my guide. This is good advice after some basic fundamentals are established in the developing process: for example, the Golden Rule "Love your neighbor as yourself" is a basic value from which to source your views when you are forming opinion. It is important to know that you can disagree with others respectfully. To put it simply, it's called expressing a different opinion with kindness fearlessly.

Whereas there are times in everyone's life that he or she will need to rely on the assistance of another, everyone will also meet a moment when there is no assistance available by another to think for you. This is where it comes to your experiences to carry you ahead. Your situation will always dictate an instruction but should you rely on your experience to instruct you, you won't make so many personal mistakes. Reform your reality reform your life is another way to examine how you are processing and interacting with what you know to be self evident and what you don't know to be evident. Forming opinions should not be based on anything other than your heart's inclinations. Chances are your heart holds the truth to your views.

There are many people who do not form opinions; instead, they just accept other people's opinion. This is not the way to be out front. You are out front when you are in front of opinion with reality that works for you. Emerging reality that works best for you is that you become aware of yourself in relation to your needs. Believe it or not, needs change from person to person, family to family, circumstance to circumstance, and generation to generation. Equally important, forming your values around your needs is an automatic for your mind. If there is a time when it's not, likely it is because you are thinking too much about other opinions weighing in on your personal view. What I have learned about myself is that I tend to over think matters when I start to weigh too many other opinions instead of letting my heart weigh matters.

With regard to becoming an informed person, you should not take for granted the wisdom entrusted to your heart. Go there and listen each time before you form opinions. Your heart knows what is best for you like nothing else does entirely.

Reforming your reality to embrace your heart is reforming your life from those minds inside of your mind. In the case of having no experience to visit in your mind in order to form an opinion, your heart is hardwired to guide you with the experience needed. It's designed that way. No one can really explain this brilliance.

> Your heart holds
> the intuition to
> guide you when
> there is no
> experience to
> lead you.

Reality is the result of listening to your heart for guidance. Everyone's life is different; therefore, opinions and values differ. Over a period of time maturity is reached, and we all can rely on our hearts to lead us to clarity about every issue in life. All of the issues of life are contained within our hearts. Thus, it's best to be consulted when experience is absent and thinking becomes overwhelming. In the final analysis of forming opinion with regard to values, it's best that you don't over think your decisions. Your heart is there to discern the nature of all things whereas your mind is there to analyze all things.

You must know the difference between your mind and your heart in terms of aligning yourself with accuracy that eliminates inner turmoil. Should not know how to separate your heart from your mind and your mind from your heart, it can easily result in your having regret about what you could have, should have, and would have been if you had known the contrast. Let this little insight work miracles in your life when you are asked to weigh in on opinions. You find that you are simply a genius without ever having to make yourself one just by knowing the difference between the role of your heart and mind.

Live by listening
to your heart rather
than your opinion.

17

Think Twice Before Being Susceptible to All Pressures

Reforming your life should never be anticipated by pressure. So many things could go wrong when you are pressured into doing anything. Governing your mind is not something that needs to be done forcefully.

Life usually is formed in the process of nine months although there are exceptions. Everything that is worth your thinking about it is worth thinking twice. It can reassure you of making hasty choices, decisions, and conclusions. Your life is something that you should take seriously. Also, you should make sure that others take your participation seriously. You need time to properly reorganize your life. It's best done one thought at a time.

Pressure beyond one thought at a time can cause mental breakdown. This can lead to confusion and much guessing. When you guess too regularly, you are probably susceptible to a timeline or pressure. Your future tends to breakdown when you put under pressure what wants to manifest for you naturally. More frequently than not, pressure leads to repetition of mistakes and breakdown. The true reformer of his or her life knows that patience is the paradigm with which to do it, especially when it comes to letting your future unfold. You should not either breakdown because of pressure or create irrational timelines. Both pressure and deadlines, if not analyzed appropriately, will deplete you of your hope. Patience prevents breakdown. The key to healthy and ethical reform is patience. You can manifest all things efficiently if you are patient. If you don't use patience all the way when pressure is there to entice you, it may result in your making the wrong decision.

Pressure is not so much designed for impulsive actions as much as it demonstrates impatience in a situation that needs good judgment. Your future deserves your best judgment. In order not to abort your dreams, you cannot allow your dreams to be put under pressure. Should you do so, it means that your patience is either gone or your patience isn't real.

Never let your temper
expire the dream of
your future.

If your impatience caused you to abandon your dream, it means that you were susceptible to pressure; therefore, you didn't examine your patience. How bad you want anything in life depends on the existence of your patience.

Patience is timeless and rich!
Its boundlessness is
all encompassing!
Patience is the
immutability of success.

Analyze carefully every decision before making it. Discern the outcome of both your decisions and choice beforehand. You will find that after a series of revisiting them before acting upon them that you become more cautious with your destiny than reckless. Reforming your life and starting it over again where it is necessary to do so starts with changing your reality to accommodate patience rather than being susceptible to pressure. Thinking twice about something does not mean that you hesitate to respond, instead, that you are sure that you want to respond the way that you feel confirmed from your inner dialogue.

Being susceptible in life is the same as being put together by life. Being accountable for your life means that you put your life together thoughtfully, patiently, and responsibly; any time that you are rushing with your life, you are speeding up chances for things to form untimely. For instance, have you ever cooked your dinner too fast, especially fried food? Chances are that your meat portion would not be as tender as if it would have been prepared timely. This is what your future turns out to be when you are susceptible to pressure to act uniformed. It has been my experience that whenever I am uniformed, it has been usually that I did not do my due diligence to observe it closely.

I advise anyone before reforming his or her life to first try to observe the damage that impatience can do. Impatience can ruin your life.

In your patience,

you possess your
soul - St. Luke 21:19.

To add a thought, patience surrenders your soul from unrest. Better is patience after you have reformed your reality and your wants fall into place. What I have learned about successful people is that their success is the product of infinite patience. On the other hand, for those of us on our way to success, "Let patience have its perfect work, that we may see perfection entirely wanting for nothing." James 5: 7

This, I say, patience has no expiration! Intellectual materialization comes gradually. Observe carefully every option when concluding your judgment about yourself. Don't become irascible because of pressure.

Pressure assumes force by something influential or someone compelling such as a moral force on your mind or will. It's the worst condition to analyze carefully your emotions and feelings. It's like being under urgent demand to compete with someone's over empowering influence. This is not fair to you ever! A balanced life is filled with self control, the essence of reforming your reality and your life.

Over the period of 40 years, I have come to the conclusion that my patience can work better than being too ambitious. It is essential to let your mind work for you. When under pressure, you begin to work for it rather than its working for you. When working for you, your mind is an operator. It dispatches all data in the brain box, so to speak. It knows what data belongs where.

Under pressure it can malfunction, and malfunction leads to incorrect judgment. Going forward with your life means that you fix mistakes caused by frustration and pressure. Learning to be calm even when you should be under pressure will lead to smart thinking and better outcomes in your life. It's what all people really want for their lives. Keep in mind that your mind works for you and not you for your mind. It knows! You can see its intuition work for you best when you keep it from getting overwhelmed by pressure.

Reform Your Reality Reform Your Life

18

Accept People; Be Comfortable With Yourself

Long before anyone understood the importance of respect for each other, many lost their lives. History holds the vaults filled with expired people because of lack of respect for each other. Reform, therefore, was much needed for the concept of mutuality and uniqueness to bring us to where we are today in the world. One of the hardest things you may have to do in your life is accept people for who they are and what they represent and at the same time maintain being comfortable with who you are and what you represent which may be totally opposite of them. It has been the most challenging thing for some. All people are unique. All people have different dreams, aspirations, and destinies.

You were created to be like no person that you know. The goal for all lives should be that each of us strives to be the best at what each of us is designed to be. No two people have the same assignment; therefore, no two people should have the same path entirely.

There are differences. Today, difference is viewed in a new vein. It can be rejected, but it does not have to be accepted for it to be the right way for you. You, therefore, must embrace it as being comfortable with yourself if you are unlike most people that you know. Comfortable with self is a divine gift within itself. Everyone wants you to accept his or her recipe for your future. Be advised that you are not to be so susceptible to all those tongues.

Instead, follow your identity of individuality to the end of your life. If you are not an orthodox person, there is nothing at all wrong with you. Do not embrace the tongues of many. Accept them, but do not change what you have in you.

You were put here with a higher purpose inside of you if your unorthodoxy challenges the readiness of the current global culture.

Being an unorthodox person simply means that you've been given a different destiny code from the normal. Because many people use the name of God to embrace orthodox religion, it defuses people from being open minded to uniqueness. Most people have not figured out the difference between God and being blind to reality. God is awareness of what is real. To put it simply, God is a unique Spirit. Who can argue that or refute it? Here is the lesson in my point: commonality is good in the respect that we share some basic need for existence, but being unique is a basic need for progression of life. What you will discover about yourself is that there has always been something within you that wanted to come forth quite differently from the way that you are used to seeing. It's like this for everyone. No matter what you do that you have seen, there is an intuition that is uniquely part of your thinking that wants you to improve all things about your ways. This intuition is distant from the orthodox way.

If you have it, you know it's a real passion with an intention to excel. Such passion itself is a type of seed containing the blueprint of what wants to emerge in the form of intellect and invention. If in your life it is not sown differently from the orthodox, you never really come to being comfortable with yourself. In a very germane way of putting it, "If someone has an issue with your uniqueness, it's that you are too unorthodox and the person with whom you are communicating isn't ready to embrace a new you." Everyone should be different! Let your comfort be established in your individuality. Unique people hold the destiny for the future. They carry within themselves the outpouring direction for dreams to be manifested.

In any unique mentality, there are wits that know what wants to come forth. This possesses an outpouring of abundance when it comes to intervention. Reforming your reality to accommodate your life's being unique from most people around you suggests that you become comfortable in your own skin. When you are comfortable with you, there is a type of glory that you carry. Such glory is not counterfeit; neither can it be counterfeited. You become the focus of attention always, and you are rarely forgotten. What is important to know is that when you accept yourself being who you really are, then that is really when you can accept other people's being themselves. There should be within us a non judgmental consciousness. What is more, it will grow our tolerance to appreciate uniqueness, and it will reorganize our perception to embrace its beauty, therefore, erasing any polarization that keeps the world from coming forth with unborn and unseen awareness to come.

Reforming your life
starts with your
reality about yourself.

The question everyone should ask himself/herself is why does the world fear an unorthodox intuition? What you are going to find out is that people in control of things that happen in the world are afraid of a different movement in the world with which they aren't in control! Control has a subtle intention to take, deceive, manipulate, and kill. Reforming your reality is taking control of life from those things to which you once lay captive.

Overall, delineations between accepting people and being comfortable with self come to full circle once all of us get rid of the fear of not being the one to control everything. It is when you don't accept people, that they become resentful, hateful, and dreadful. They then, display the worst imaginable morality. No form of legislation seems to keep their emotions under control. The same is true about self. A self deprived, in any way, ultimately leads to ruin of that self and often others. It is time to come to the realization that whereas we are unique, we still must respect each other's uniqueness of values and paths of life. Things to do today to accept people and be comfortable with self begin and end with love for others and self. The greatest contribution that your life can embrace is your individuality. What you are, no one else can duplicate. Appreciate it, be thankful for it, and do something with it!

Reform Your Reality Reform Your Life

19

Be True to Oneself Instead of People Pleasing

One of the hardest traits to master about yourself is that you should never be unstable about what you really believe about yourself and what you want to see for others. It could be simple if there were not so many opinions about what you hold to be true and self evident. This is not the truth for everyone. There are some people who are straight forward with being true to themselves. It is believed to be the best and/or most rewarding way to establish a peaceful life. Unfortunately, not all people have the courage to take a stand for their inner truths. Most likely, they are not forthcoming with their intentions and they just lie! This creates the worst condition for everyone. No illusion can be justified; instead, truth extinguishes an illusion.

Reforming your reality so that you reform your life starts with being absolutely truthful with yourself about everything.

Being truthful with yourself is the beginning of erasing mistakes in your life; therefore, you can begin to see real changes take place in it. Your life and the life of everyone with whom you interact take on new outcomes as a result of your honesty. Sometimes all of us have not focused on the nature of the damage that we can cause by not being true to ourselves and others involved. It is the case many times when we forsake our own wishes to accommodate other people's wishes that causes setbacks to our real dreams and passion.

Often, the images of a particular life style and/or status with which you seek to imitate rob you of the life engineered according to God's blueprint in your heart. Pleasing anything and anyone is a mistake in consciousness because it does not ask you to be true to yourself which has to be first reckoned. If you do observe your own motions within in terms of satisfaction, they will find you and demand your attention. The sooner you give them your attention, you will prevent setbacks from occurring in your life. If you look real closely into your heart, the very truth about what you are consciously unaware of exists. Haven't you decided with others about things that you had little or no knowledge about? This is likely the reason for some of the "people pleasing" on our positions about things. What is more, very few people side with others because of friendship(s) and some please others for the love of what they either have or what they can provide.

Y ou will miss out

on a totally fulfilled life

without including your

heart's totally being represented by the truth in it.

Reality is total identification and reckoning with yourself. It is as if you are looking into your heart to find those things inconsistent with truth and correcting them all at the same time. After you have discovered happiness for yourself first, then it is up to those people who genuinely accept you for who and what you are instead of your suppressing your heart.

Whereas you may not have been careful to fully understand why you are what you are and why you think the way that you do, your heart knows how to instruct your mind better than your thinking. In your heart are the issues of your life; therefore, the world itself has been set into your heart to experience all that you behold of it! Check with your heart before you go changing too much about yourself for others in your life. You will find that being unique is very important because uniqueness sparks curiosity

Curiosity peaks interest!

All is right about being

you just the way you are.

Destiny is to be structured.

Did you know that? It could be that everything in error with your life is the result of not being who you are designed to be. Each person has value and significance. All people have different features but they are to be respected the same for their individuality. Could it be that envy is the cause of needing to be pleased and/or suppressing someone else's individuality? Reforming your reality about what you are is the starting place for an abundant life and therefore, being true to it suggests that you come away from the habit of conforming to others' opinion about what you should or shouldn't be!

You are the expression
that cannot be duplicated;
therefore, be what you
should be—true to yourself.

You will discover that it makes all the difference with your life. Many people never get a chance to live a self- actualizing life during their experience with life. It's true that an absence of truth about yourself causes you to end up living a defeated life with loss of opportunity to be happiest in life. Don't stand on the side line of life wondering what might have been and what could have been with your life, rather make sure that it is being lived in truth with passion, individuality, and creativity. Let your future emerge in the now.

Reform your life
by reforming your
reality of truth
about yourself.

It is the best advice for well-being and happiness. It is time for you to be happy! No one should be given permission to have an opinion of it as far as you should be concerned. Just live respecting others as yourself and being as loving, caring, and sharing with all the characteristics that come with you. What really matters most is how you interpret yourself. Should you not be true to yourself, you become displeased with yourself. This is not what anyone should want; thus, it proves one to be unstable and/or double minded. It affects your well-being in ways that can be emotionally debilitating if not corrected over a period of time. It can turn into sadness, madness, and delusion. All of which are mentally challenging. The outcome associated with establishing your integrity is peace within!

Reform Your Reality Reform Your Life

20

Believe Yourself to Be Creative

You have everything you need to be creative. Believing yourself to be creative is the discovery of your own personal abundance! It's extremely necessary that you discover it! The image of your makeup consists of parts. First, you are spirit possessing dominion in the earth. Second, you are a living body in the earth. In this image, you are the body containing the spirit of dominion on the earth unlike any other living being. Your spirit contains intuition beyond anything that you can fathom. The intuition of your spirit is the mighty entity that you carry within your body. It is like DNA. It contains certain knowledge about all that is and that is to come. The spirit within you is the beginning data of creation itself.

It's typical of a treasure chest holding all the mysteries to everything. It is yours to open if you will. All that you find in it is yours. You are the one with all of the abilities that come with power. Your entire success in life depends on it. The components of creativity are spiritual, physical, and psychological. You will know that you have no limits to what you can achieve after you have reality about where your boundary is relative to your habitation. Surely, if you are serious about being creative, you first need to come to terms with what you've been given to inhabit— the earth! All that you can do will be done in the earth; thus, there is no purpose for being creative beyond your earthly habitation. All of your labor is profitable to you in the earth. You will enjoy your labor on the earth. You have the only visible tools with which to manifest things on the earth. They are intuition, psychology, and the physical. Being a creative person means that you align yourself with an intention to work your intuition with your mind and your mind with your body in harmony to apply yourself to a purpose.

There shall
be nothing
impossible to you.

It does take time to awaken to the power. This means that there will be certain knowledge that you will have to seek, but it does not mean that it's not obtainable. On the contrary, it means that you must gather it. There are times that you will find that other people gather certain knowledge before you do. So, consulting with others is helpful. Keep in mind, all of us possess the same spirit and all of us have its potential.

The belief that people are creative was the assignment given to the first man that lived and thus, all of us. Believing in yourself does not mean that you are self righteous as some suppose. On the contrary, righteousness and belief are defined differently. Righteousness is the tenant of the morality, and belief is the tenant of the mind. Should you believe yourself to be creative, all things are possible to you! Believing in yourself means that you understand yourself. It does not mean that you do not believe in God. On the contrary, it means that you don't separate yourself from the image of God. In the image of God, you are that vivid description and representation. Formed exactly in the likeness, there is not another being that resembles its living power. To put it simply, all you can really be interpreted as is the personification of the Creator.

This suggests that you come to agreement with being the Creator's breath contained in a body that lives on the earth! You were placed here to inhabit the life that you were given for the purpose of being a steward and or keeper of the earth. Seeing yourself being separated from the Creator's form is to be seen as lost or in some way to be distant from reality consistent with the

Image in Whose you are. In the same way, everything is seen and experienced by you as with God. The stories of the ones enlightened have no different consummation no matter their names. All come to the same final truth—God is Spirit and the Spirit contained in you! The awareness of God is the awareness of consciousness of that Spirit being your Source of creation. Such awakening is accessible to all that seek to understand it.

Let not your mind complicate creativity. It's a simple notion. Just align your spirit, body, and intention in unity and accept who you are, from where you originated, and all that you are capable. All people are apt to the Creator's imagination. From the first person until present, all people should be seen as a reproduction of the Creator and sculpted in its likeness. Thus, you will find that everyone has an opinion about the Creator's imagination. For some, they suggest that a mental picture of the Creator's imagination is not present to behold. I would agree that this entity is not visible, but I disagree with the fact that it does not exist. It exists within the makeup of your spirit which is not visible. It is contained in your form. Such data was transferred to your imagination and exemplified through your mind.

In order for the Creator's imagination to be duplicated, the suggestion consistent with reality is that it was placed within your form to produce likeness of its kind. What is more evident about the creative imagination within you is it's the symbol of creation. It typifies mentally how everything was envisioned before it was formed. I might add a thought, it behaves without limitation!

Does that mean that you have no limits to which with you are capable? You can determine that by your acceptance of what you choose to believe. When it comes to the Creator's intuition, it, too, is in your makeup. The spirit which contains your life is vast. Its depth represents a set of mental pictures or images. Also, it uses vivid or figurative language to represent objects, actions, or ideas.

Putting it simply, the spirit entity of your makeup is the Creator's intuition. It is the ability to confront and deal with reality creatively! A valid description of your having the Creator's intuition is seen in the fact that you create daily impressions about things before you experience them, and most times relative to your intuition your knowledge of it beforehand is derived from intuition rather than experience. Surely, the

Creator is intuitive or else no creation could exist. You are the expressed image of the Creator's intuition and this truth is sustained both by reason and evidence.

Reforming your reality
to embrace your
Creator's intuition
immediately reforms
the outcomes in
your life.

Let's not overlook the Creator's consciousness. It, too, is contained in the entity of the Creator's Spirit in you. So much is to be said about the Creator's conscious. It is also contained in the spirit in you. Your consciousness resembles the Creator's consciousness. It is the exact reflection of it. Should you awaken it, to your discovery, it contains wisdom, knowledge, insightfulness, awareness, and ultimate reality. The consciousness of the Creator within the entity of the spirit in you possesses an awareness of all that was, is, and to come. To characterize it, such description encompasses having an awareness of environment, existence, and life! Such consciousness, if awake, is the component of waking awareness perceptible to you at any given instance to identify everything.

The state or condition of being fully awakened to the Creator's consciousness is a condition of achieving greater awareness of all that is needed, relative to all that belongs in the world in order to fulfill the potential of the environment, existence, and life. While the scientific community may delve into the Creator's consciousness more than the normal population, it is for all people to experience. The purpose for which the Creator formed you in its image is that you experience, participate, illustrate and connect with creative awareness. With that being said, the Creator's awareness exists, too, in the makeup of its spirit within you. Every invention on the earth was derived out of creative awareness. Believing yourself to be creative can awaken you to escalated awareness. Such clarity restores the sick, restores the doubtful, restores the weak, restores lost belonging, and revives identity inferiority. God is your spirit; God is your lifelong partner!

Being creative is all about how you identify yourself with every aspect of existence marked by fully waking to the spirit of God in you. It's most needed for any person pursuing life. The person most recognized for possessing the Creator's power with himself was Jesus. His words,

"He that believes on me, the things I've done, you can do also; even greater things" are so consistent with the reality that we need to be creative. You are capable of greatness to any degree. I suggest that you not limit yourself to restriction. Don't think that you are limited because your body will someday not be needed to carry you.

Your body is typical of a tool box. Each component of your body is a tool which your spirit uses to get things done. There is another glorious body waiting for the spirit you contain says Jesus! I know that you would want it described. I too! We will have to wait for that knowing. What is important for now is the earth age. You need not to look beyond here and now in terms of what you are capable of doing. The reality that Jesus could duplicate creative works is much more illustrative of the Spirit of God than anything. Undoubtedly, He believed that you could do the same! There are others having demonstrated and emulated the Creator, too! Now it is your opportunity.

The Creator's mind
is contained in the
spirit entity within you.

If it were not, there would be no you. The burden of truth about it is that you let it mature! For a long time, haven't you wondered how God is the curiosity of people, but people are skeptical being what God is in form? Today, let the wisdom contained in the entity of the spirit within you manifest itself to you wholly, and it will solve every curiosity that you have about everything! You, like Jesus, are capable of such things He's already done. If you really applied yourself to inhabit the Creator's mind to do creative things, you could do them. Granted, you might have to erase your ego, pride, selfishness, and reasoning for which you think you ought to be. Instead, lose your will and allow the Spirit of God in you to behave without any willingness to be an independent creature. The Creator's mind within the entity of Jesus' body contained abilities so creative that it tends to be unbelievable that you could do the same.

The truth is that being creative does not have to be demonstrated in one form. There are many ways to be creative. While Jesus demonstrated creativity with words and energy, today it is being done by other technological means so that all know the power of the spirit contained in us! Jesus' creativeness was illustrated by the following.

- Water changed to wine, Jn. 2:9.
- The Nobleman's son, Jn. 4:46.
- Draught of fish, Lu. 5:6.
- Demoniac in the synagogue, Mk. 1:26; Lu. 4:35.
- Peter's mother-in-law healed, Mt. 8:14; Mk. 1:31; Lu. 4:38.
- Cleansing the leper, Mt. 8:3; Mk. 1:41; Lu. 5:13.
- Paralytic, Mt. 9:2; Mk. 2:3; Lu. 5:18.
- Impotent man healed, Jn. 5:5.
- Withered hand, Mt. 12:10; Mk. 3:1; Lu. 6:6.
- Centurion's servant, Mt. 8:5; Lu. 7:2.
- Raising the widow's son, Lu. 7:11.
- Demoniac, Mt. 12:22; Lu. 11:14.

- Tempest stilled, Mt. 8:26; Mk. 4:39; Lu. 8:24
- Demoniacs of Gadara, Mt. 8:28; Mk. 5:1; Lu. 8:26
- Raising of Jairus' daughter, Mt. 9:18; Mk. 5:42; Lu. 8:41.
- Issue of Blood, Mt. 9:20; Mk. 5:25; Lu. 8:43.
- Blind men, Mt. 9:27.
- Demoniac, Mt. 9:32.
- Feeding five thousand, Mt. 14:15; Mk. 6:41; Lu. 9:12; Jn. 6:5.
- Walking on the sea, Mt. 14:25; Mk. 6:49; Jn. 6:19
- Daughter of Syrophenician, Mt. 15:22; Mk. 7:25.
- Feeding the four thousand, Mt. 15:32; Mk. 8:8.
- Deaf and dumb healed, Mk. 7:33.

- Blind man, Mk. 8:23.
- Lunatic child, Mt. 17:14; Mk. 9:26; Lu. 9:37
- Tribute money, Mt. 17: 24.
- Healing the Ten lepers, Lu. 17: 12.
- Blind man, Jn. 9:1.
- Lazarus raised, Jn. 11.
- Healing the woman with the spirit of infirmity, Lu. 13: 11
- Man with dropsy, Lu. 14: 2.
- Blind men, Mt. 20: 30; Mk. 10: 46.
- Cursing the fig tree, Mt. 21: 19.
- Healing Malchus, Lu. 22:51
- Second draught of fish, Jn. 21: 6.
- Raising upon His resurrection, Lu. 24: 6; Jn. 10: 18.
- Appearing to his disciple (Paul), Acts 9.

Jesus used his creativity to do these things with an intention to inspire you to do new things. Though you may be amazed that such things were done, are you at least curious about how to be creative, too? The fact is that the Creator's curiosity is also contained in the entity of the spirit in you. No one truly can say I am not curious about creativity. The creative process in some way is to examine curiosity and let it hand over its intelligence so that you record its findings. Nothing can take you on a journey filled with every detail that you envision like that of curiosity. With this said, curiosity expands your intuitive reach for evidence needed in your life.

Among the greatest men of scientific wisdom was Albert Einstein. It is said that he identified the driving force in his lifelong research to be curiosity. In some way, undoubtedly, all people are propelled to press forcibly into wisdom they don't have about all the things they want to know. The Creator's curiosity in your spirit is there to guide and direct you to new inventions in your life. Thus, it behaves with an intention that penetrates the hidden wisdom from the invisible state to create or produce visible manifestations, often expressively. To put it simply, within everyone there lies an inquisitive ingenuity waiting to be demonstrated. Lastly, there exists in the spirit entity of the spirit in you the Creator's intention.

The creative intention within you is a course of action that wants to flow in your mind after you have given yourself a task. That same intention is an aim that guides your actions! It knows your plans and, therefore, it's designed to help you achieve the goal set for you. Something unique happens for you when you allow the creative intention to flow through your mind, your hands, your feet, your gifts, and your entire life. The uniqueness of it is that it strengthens the idea of your resolution and determination! Make it your intention to be creative!

21

Become Better Than Predicted

People in this generation are not the same people in every generation. Each generation has different needs, assignments, and livelihood. Therefore, reality that is effective has to be relevant in terms of means and support for this generation. The purpose of each generation has been clearly defined. Every generation is given the task to improve the mistakes of the previous generation with God and man. What is more, it's time for you to launch into the deep task of higher awareness. In the area of doing greater things, such as recovering yourself from the ills of the previous generation's ignorance, you were born to be greater. In some ways, but not all ways, the previous generation's failing to equip this generation with knowing how to shape potential and possibility was left to you, so that you awaken to your own greatness.

You must not fail to bring forth clarity of greater depth in awareness needed to recover your pain today from the ills of society. If you attempt to heal your sickness, rise from the dead mentally, and pattern yourself after greatness rather than what is predicted of you, then a reawakening of the Christ consciousness can appeal to you. This current generation will see you different from others in terms of what you achieve in your life. Take a good look at how you may be able to improve yourself with ways to redefine the potential unborn to people. Spend some quiet time observing how to correct your mistakes. It will prove to advance your awareness of self. Get serious about mentoring yourself psychologically, socially, and financially with an emphasis to empower yourself to fulfill your unique purpose in life!

Your very own passion has to be consistent with the living cutting edge; therefore, harness your mind toward greatness! Think about what it means to be great. Here are the words of the Christ, "If ye believe on me, the things I do, you can do also; even greater." I believe that GREATNESS is the challenge of the generation today! People in this generation want their churches, schools, institutions of higher learning, medical communities, technology partners, and governmental entities to offer them relevant events and activities leading to the accumulation of awareness, understanding, and knowledge that self empower them!

They want to take part and/or share in a vision consistent with bringing forth their full potential instead of cultural baggage! They want examples of realism that have outcomes of proof to embrace rather than promised prolonged perpetual waiting! With all that you have been given from your parents and other teachers in history, appealing to people differently from what is expected of you can redefine greatness about you.

Greatness is the remarkable
degree of awareness
of what has to come forth
about you in the now and,
to some degree, a knowing
of what you ought to do with
regard to challenges that
you face.

I don't doubt that greatness comes through connection to God! Live by no specific predictions; instead, live after the passion of your heart. It will prove to be most rewarding. Each morning that you awake, take the first ten minutes of consciousness to examine what's given to your mind to register. There will be times that you get up in the morning and nothing that makes sense about either your dreams or thoughts is clear, but there will be other times when after you have either prayed or you were waiting for direction to come as a result of yearning instructions, it shall be placed in your mind field how to go about it before you ever get out of bed. What I have learned about greatness is that I really do not know the timing of its precision; rather I follow after it precisely!

> **The reality of greatness transforms your ability to go beyond what others predict of you.**

With this being said, greatness contains insightfulness of the harmony of your mind, body, and spirit. You will behave greatly when you come full circle with yourself and your calling. Becoming better than predicted intuitively suggests that you are freed from the manipulation of all the minds within your mind which led you by the hand before your awakening came. Such awakening of liberation holistically—mind, body, and spirit—is really the tenant of your personal meaning of life. Reforming your reality to align with greatness will place you in front of creative ways that manifest new thinking and new construction with your life calibrating the power of a shift in consciousness in order that you do greater things than expected of you!

I am reminded of story of little boy who proved to be greater than predicted. This little boy was born to an average family. His mother gave him the nickname Diamond. He never paid much attention to that nickname early on. He had an average life with all of the basic necessities in place for him to survive. His family gave him lots of love, but they didn't have money to give him. He, like the average kid, was given some of the things that he wanted during special times in his life: his birthday and Christmas. He did the average things little boys do in their lives. Diamond was taught to pray; thus, he became God conscious as he imagined His God.

Diamond was the type of boy who was a dreamer. He carried vision within himself. As a teenager, he appeared to be before his time in terms of wisdom and maturity although he was a little timid with it. At the age of 18, he was baptized in Jesus' Name, and at the age of 19 he was inspired to carry the vision of Jesus within himself as his own. Diamond had no experience with ministry because he had not been raised under a priest.

He did have his mother and great grandmother as believers in the church to assist him only to pray and God would provide him direction. So he did just that. Diamond continued as a young minister carrying in his heart dreams that no one in his family shared. He became the first in his family to achieve master and doctorate degrees. He became the first priest in his immediate family.

Thus, he did lead his family to God. Starting with his sisters, cousins, and grandmother, he baptized all of them. Diamond eventually became the first author in his family. By the time he was 40, he had written 4 meaningful books. He was the first entrepreneur in his family. Also, he was the first church planter in his family, and he was the first not to fear being unique from the family brand and prediction. In some ways Diamond became greater than predicted by his family. He leads them today, not as one they knew, but as one that is new to them. He knows that he is challenging to them, but he also knows that he has to raise their level of consciousness. Diamond finally received awareness of why his mother called him Diamond as a nickname. Diamond symbolizes an inner acute angle used as a gemstone to cut into other objects to establish form.

For Diamond, it meant that he understood that it was he who had to experience a change from his natural self so that he could reestablish the form which his family needed to become awakened to the Christ consciousness, thus becoming better than predicted. Maybe, you are the one for whom the world is waiting to be its example of greatness. Challenge yourself to become better than predicted!

Epilogue

I have been inspired to write this book with an emphasis to bring out the best in you. I wish you the best read. As I conclude the book, my mind informs me that every person serious about reforming himself has so many great minds as examples. Here are my last words in this manuscript. People have always shaped the world by their lifestyles. Today, many lives, legacies, and sacrifices prove to have been those that changed the world. Choosing your lifestyle is most important. It has the potential to shape the world! Several factors involved in shaping the mindset of the world include awareness of outcomes of your choices. Achievement is a choice. Your options in life are choices. It is within you to determine what your life will be and how you will be remembered in history. What is more, one cannot be bound when one understands that his or her choices bring him or her to all that can be experienced in life. No one's fate in life is unchangeable from the time of birth. An alternative is always available via the making of choices. What I have discovered about myself is that I prefer not to leave my fate in the hands of anyone; rather I will explore it to possibility.

The liberty to choose your life implies broadly the freedom to emphasize between possibilities and nothingness. Living in the socio-political climate of America supports individual choices for which I am grateful! No matter the social culture, politics, and laws in civilizations around the world, all rules of enforcement from the very beginning of human being existence support that people should have choices. There may be remnants of totalitarianism in remote places in the world today, but eventually the will to be free to choose the lifestyle one wants and/or his or her fate in life will always prove to be stronger than policies restricting choices. One's lifestyle is to be considered by the territory on, within, or in oneself!

Choices are similar to options with spin-offs. No one limits one's fate but oneself! Choices are there to identify your thinking patterns; therefore, you should observe them daily! With this being said, you can determine the lifestyle you look forward to in the world. Life really takes on new meaning when it is unrestricted! Some of my favorite themes for thought are "Fate is not in the stars to hold our destiny but in us"—William Shakespeare; "Destiny is not a

matter of chance; it is a matter of choice"—
William Jennings Bryan; "If you have faith as
a grain of mustard seed and shall say unto
this mountain...nothing shall be impossible
unto you"—Jesus Christ; "The choice to
make is one that you know can advance
virtue and wholesomeness in your life"—
Dwayne Gavin; "All we are is the result of
what we have ever thought"—Siddhartha
Gautama; "I have a dream"—Rev. Dr.
Martin Luther King, Jr.; and "Lifestyle is a
choice and so is achievement"—Dwayne
Gavin.

So today, let the world pattern itself
after the Late Rev. Dr. Martin Luther King,
Jr., and all those historical mental trends of
the greatest minds of all time as we choose
our lives! The hope is that all lives
contribute reform to the way it can best
shape the world for those who may come
behind them. All the ways to success are by

the choices we make. What I have opened my mind up to see is that the Creator uses our hands to erect most things, our faith to move mountains, our minds to inspire, and our choice of lifestyle to constantly advance the world being shaped!

Summary

This book is about how emerging reality reforms life. It contains much of the insights of the self and God within Whom the self inhabits. The wisdom placed in the book is the insightfulness bringing people out from mind control of all things to merely a reflection of one's experiences and expressions, emerging as a being empowered with new possibilities, potential, and consciousness.

Much of the content of the book are ideals about how to reform yourself consciously. Throughout the book is the reality of empowering you with awareness, recovering you with ultimate understanding, and equipping you with cutting-edge knowledge for a grander life and success via techniques about how to rearrange your thoughts, feelings, and perception of life. A great deal of energy

Summary

that permeates the book focused on confronting oneself in terms of choices, beliefs, cultural norms, mind control, and freedom. Almost every attempt is to bring you closer to the ultimate reality.

It highly embraces liberated actions for experiencing life freely, responsibly, and intentionally while at the same time letting your meaning of life emerge from the vast experiences that make it. With this in mind, reform your reality to see beyond the resistance of knowing yourself to a grander degree by understanding how to develop yourself to reach total awareness of those things occurring in your life. Sections of the book bring to the front a brand new way of reconstructing your reality using the power of shift in consciousness to experience desired results. Ultimately, the reality of the book is an understanding of how to become insightful about transforming your life.

Bibliography

King James Reference Bible

Copyright 2000, Zondervan Publishing,

Grand Rapids, Michigan, U.S.A.

Library of congress Card Number 00-75836

The American heritage College *dic.tion.ar.y*

Third Edition

Copyright 1993 by Houghton Mifflin Company

Triumph

Dwayne Gavin

Copyright 2012, DG Publishing House,

Tallahassee, Florida, U.S.A.

Library of Congress Number 2012912312

Other Books by Dr. Dwayne Gavin

MORALITY- The book contains many secrets to enhance you to reach your fullest potential via a shift in consciousness. Wisdom from across the earth comes together in unity within the book as it contains integration of spirituality, psychology, and philosophy. The book has no religious prejudice. The focus of the book is to heighten global human being with an emphasis on higher reality.

CHOOSE YOUR LIFE- Choose Your Life is the wisdom of generational truths. The book contains thousands of years of quotes from people who have shaped the world with a global awareness. The work offers an approach to attain new outcomes in one's life in a very relevant way in a modern, fast-paced culture. The book offers logical, philosophical, and psychological approaches to decision making.

TRIUMPH- <u>Triumph</u> reminds us of how to enhance ourselves in every way. The depth of individual triumph is the result of heightened reality. The book is a tool that suggests what life can be holistically. With its emphasis on consciousness, it supports an urgency to reach an escalated awareness in order to experience the basic shifts in consciousness. The intention of the book is to offer an alternative approach to a simple and blissful life unique from the predictions of life being fixed. All in all, Triumph is a waking up of self.

See Dr. Dwayne Gavin's Awareness for Life Broadcast © sponsored by DG PUBLISHING Press. For Dwayne Gavin books, see dwaynegavin.com. Dr. Dwayne Gavin's teachings help you reach your fullest potential to create extraordinary results in your life, career, business, and organization. His insight on the fundamentals of coaching is a tool to assist you to mentally recreate yourself to produce greater manifestations to happen in your life. Dr. Gavin's book titled CHOOSE YOUR LIFE is one of two manuals for motivational speaking, coaching, teaching, counseling, and inner empowerment.

Reflections by Michael Henley
(Valdosta, GA)

While learning true awareness of the Christ consciousness through the teachings, preaching, and examples of Dr. Gavin, I am in Christ living today to its fullest extent- When tomorrow comes, Christ and I will prove yesterday wasn't an accident!

Reflections by Frank and Selena Bryant (Valdosta, GA)

I have seen Dr. Gavin's diligence over a number of years prepare him for writing this book. It is awesome to be a support base with him and others who are Global Christian Church partners.

Reflections by Jacqueline Harper

(Quitman, GA)

I question not my destiny of being at an earthly master's foot for learning that which the Master of all things would have me know. The journey has truly been one of awareness, understanding, and knowledge; forgiveness of self and others; ridding oneself of cultural baggage; and experiencing true worship realizing that perfection comes only through Jesus Christ our Savior, Who alone is righteous!

Reflections by Mattlyn Henley

(Valdosta, GA)

To God be the glory. As God has placed us together as family, I am blessed to have a young man of God as my shepherd. You truly are concerned about both our physical and spiritual well being. For that I am truly grateful.

Reflections by James Wright

(Valdosta, GA)

I love the Global Christian Church Family. I am being healed by Dr. Gavin's teachings. I have learned so much more than I've known about the reality of God.

Reflections by Janis Gavin

(Tallahassee, FL)

Son, continue to live one day at a time, enjoy one moment at a time accepting hardship as the pathway to peace. Keep trusting God to make all things beautiful in His time. Continue to surrender your will to God's Will. I am so proud of you!

Reflections by Joyce Crawford

(Tallahassee, FL)

Rev, without God and you in my life, I don't know where my life would be. My faith has grown as I continue to learn from your teachings. You are an inspiration to me and my sons. From all of the family in Tallahassee, Florida, "thank you and we are blessed to have you as our shepherd."

Reflections by Doris Cloud

(Tallahassee, FL)

Dr. Dwayne O. Gavin I am so proud of your wisdom, guidance, and leadership.

Reflections by Phyllis Groomes

(Tallahassee, FL)

For all you represent as pastor, visionary, and man of God, I am blessed to be a member of the Global Christian Church Family. Thank you for all of the support and everything that you've helped me with in all of my circumstances. You have always given me the best advice.

Reflections by Christine White

(Tallahassee, FL)

I am so proud of you and all of your accomplishments. I knew that you were special in the eyes of God, and I am enjoying the blessing of the Global Christian Church experience.

Reflections by Candice Jefferson

Job well done! You have made learning for me a growing experience. It is one of empowerment and new awareness. I thank God for placing me in the Global Christian Family where I may continue to grow and enhance my abilities. May God continue to bless you and the Global Christian Center, Inc.

Reflections by Dorthy Barnes
(Tallahassee, FL)

I am so happy for you. Keep doing all that God has placed in your heart!

Reflections by Tiffany Turner

I am so proud of you! Your hard work is paying off. You are a blessing to the Global Christian Church. May God continue to empower you with His blessing!

Reflections by Lakisha Nix

Thank you so much for your love, prayers and your faith. I have grown in my faith. I am happy to be part of the Global Christian Church. It helps me with my circumstances; it gives me another chance; I reign!